A Lantern in the Dark

DANIELLE BLACKWOOD

A
Lantern
in the
Dark

NAVIGATE LIFE'S CROSSROADS with
STORY, RITUAL & SACRED ASTROLOGY

Llewellyn Publications
Woodbury, Minnesota

© BK Studios

About the Author

Danielle Blackwood is a professional astrologer with more than 30 years of experience and is certified in the principles and practice of contemporary psychological astrology through world-renowned astrologer and author Erin Sullivan. Danielle is also a Registered Counseling Therapist (RCT) in private practice. Her therapeutic approach is transpersonal, archetypal, and person centered, and she holds a certificate in Jungian and post-Jungian clinical concepts through the Center of Applied Jungian Studies. Danielle has been a priestess and educator since 1994, facilitating workshops, retreats, classes, and public ritual. She is the author of *The Twelve Faces of the Goddess: Transform Your Life with Astrology, Magick, and the Sacred Feminine* (Llewellyn, 2018). Danielle is a passionate lifelong student of folklore, mythology, and depth psychology, and helping others through their rites of passage when they find themselves in a dark wood is at the heart of her work. She lives in an enchanted cottage on a tiny island on the western coast of Canada, the original lands and unceded territory of the Coast Salish peoples.

Also by Danielle Blackwood

The Twelve Faces of the Goddess: Transform Your Life with Astrology, Magick, and the Sacred Feminine

FIRST EDITION
First Printing, 2022

Book design by Colleen McLaren
Cover design by Shannon McKuhen

Llewellyn Publications is a registered trademark of Llewellyn Worldwide Ltd.

Library of Congress Cataloging-in-Publication Data (Pending)
ISBN: 9780738768687

Llewellyn Worldwide Ltd. does not participate in, endorse, or have any authority or responsibility concerning private business transactions between our authors and the public.

All mail addressed to the author is forwarded but the publisher cannot, unless specifically instructed by the author, give out an address or phone number.

Any internet references contained in this work are current at publication time, but the publisher cannot guarantee that a specific location will continue to be maintained. Please refer to the publisher's website for links to authors' websites and other sources.

Llewellyn Publications
A Division of Llewellyn Worldwide Ltd.
2143 Wooddale Drive
Woodbury, MN 55125-2989
www.llewellyn.com

Printed in the United States of America

To All Travelers Who Find Themselves at a Crossroads

May you find a lantern in the dark
To guide you home
To the infinite wonder of your Self.

May you find magic and meaning
Deftly woven into your unfolding sacred story.

And when you find yourself in a forest dark,
May you know the guidance you seek
Like an old friend who knows the way.

Disclaimer

This book is not intended to provide medical or mental health advice or to take the place of advice and treatment from your primary care provider. Readers are advised to consult their doctors or other qualified healthcare professionals regarding the treatment of their medical or mental health issues. Neither the publisher nor the author take any responsibility for any possible consequences from any treatment, action, or application of medicine, supplement, herb, or preparation to any person reading or following the information in this book.

Contents

Contents

Part 3: Full Circle

Acknowledgments

A heartfelt thank-you to all who helped make this book a reality. I would like to acknowledge everyone I have had the pleasure of working with in my practice over the years. In sharing your stories, you have each taught me something valuable, and it has been my honor and privilege to hold space for you.

Thank you to my friend Karen Clark for your support during the very first stirrings of this book over steaming cups of spiced cacao. Thank you to my friend Michelle Cunningham of Solstice Stones for collaborating on just the right stones as allies for each crossroads. And thank you to my sister Vaysha Hirsch Todorovich for brainstorming with me when I had writer's block. I am grateful for the inspiration, and our endless conversation and laughter.

So much appreciation goes out to those who read advance copies of this book and provided it with your thoughtful, eloquent support. In the order in which I received your words, I want to thank Acyuta -bhava Das (Adam Elenbaas), Steven Forrest, Renn Butler, Elizabeth Spring, Danu Forrest, Virginia Bell, Diotima Mantineia, Annwyn Avalon, Ivo Dominguez Jr., Amy Herring, Dr. Sara Cleto, Dr. Brittany Warman, Erin Sullivan, Tiffany Lazic, Stephanie Woodfield, Elena Rego, Meg Rosenbriar, Briony Silver, Kris Walherr, Seraphina Capranos, and Dr. Theodora Goss. Your generosity has touched me deeply.

An extra special thank-you to Dr. Theodora Goss and Toko-pa Turner, who so kindly granted me permission to include longer excerpts of their work in this book.

To those authors and teachers who have inspired me and shaped me into who I have become—Carl Jung, Joseph Campbell, James Hillman, Dr. Clarissa Pinkola Estés, John O'Donohue, and many others—my enduring gratitude for laying the ground to view life through an archetypal lens.

To my amazing editorial team at Llewellyn, especially Elysia Gallo and Lauryn Heineman. I couldn't do it without you!

And finally, to my husband and best friend, Jamie. Thank you for providing endless support, enthusiasm, and a safe space for my creativity to take root and blossom. We met at a crossroads, and from that day forward, you have had unwavering belief in me, for which I am eternally grateful.

At the Crossroads: Betwixt and Between

I have been called a modern-day cunningwoman and a village witch. It is true that I live in a cottage in the woods and people come to me for counsel, often of a decidedly magickal nature. My work itself is liminal, balancing between the worlds of the magickal and the mundane, as I am both professional astrologer and registered counselor. Often, the imaginary lines between the two overlap, as ultimately, my role is to determine just what medicine someone requires. And although the language of astrology is one of the main tools of my trade, I also design therapeutic rituals for my clients for everything from new beginnings to closure. I read the patterns in the seasons and tend medicinal herbs in my witch's garden according to the phases of the moon. Guiding others through their rites of passage when they find themselves in a dark wood is my passion and my life's work. I have been on this path for a very long time and have heeded the call of the Mysteries since I was old enough to perceive that there was more beneath the surface of things than is immediately apparent.

I have always been fascinated with genealogy, and several years ago I embarked on a journey through my family's origins through DNA testing and extensive family tree exploration. Through my research, I recently discovered that one of my ancestors was tried and executed for witchcraft in the Scottish Highlands during the Great Scottish Witch Hunt of 1597. She was one of what is estimated to be around 200 individuals put to death between March and October of that year and was given the small mercy of being strangled before being burned publicly. Like many of the accused, she was said to be a practitioner of folk healing. It is difficult to describe the feelings this information evoked. An overwhelming sense of sadness and heartbreak stayed with me for a long time. Even though I have identified as a witch for decades and am more than familiar with the history of oppression of women named as witches throughout Europe in the early modern period, it became tangible in a way that I did not comprehend before.

The knowledge that someone whose DNA I carry in my body was treated in such a brutal way impacted me deeply, and I found myself mourning for a woman I had never met. I silently told her how sorry I was that such an injustice had occurred and set about creating a proper end-of-life ritual for her. I have long been intrigued with the idea of genetic memory, and I question if my calling to my life's work is connected to this distant ancestor who had the unfortunate circumstance of being a healer in a time when it was a very dangerous occupation. I give humble thanks and heartfelt gratitude to live in a time when I am free to follow my calling without fearing for my life.

In my practice as a working witch, it has been my experience that clients often come to see me for the first time when they are at a crossroads. They have been going about their lives when they realize they have lost the path. They are in liminal space, betwixt and between. They are no longer who they used to be, but not quite yet who they are becoming. They may feel confused, restless, afraid, anxious, uninspired, or that they are no longer sure of who they are or what they believe. Sometimes an event has occurred in their outer life, and the proverbial rug has been pulled out from beneath them.

Crossroads by their very definition are liminal space, and the crossroads motif shows up cross-culturally throughout myth and story in every epoch. Crossroads have been a recurring motif in mythology, folklore, and folk magic since time immemorial. Numerous liminal deities are associated with crossroads, doorways, and gateways, such as Hecate, Mercury/Hermes, Terminus, Portunas, Janus, Menshen, and Legba.

When the protagonist reaches a crossroads in a story, we know that they have entered a place between the worlds: a magical realm where two worlds intersect. A place inhabited by the strange and uncanny, as well as unexpected enchantment and possibility. There is always an element of choice when one finds oneself at a crossroads. There is also an element of trust and surrender to the unknown: no matter which road you take, your life will change. In story, the protagonist often encounters a liminal being at the crossroads, a teacher of sorts whom they may or may not have expected. In the Russian folktale "Vasilisa the Beautiful," the heroine sets off into the forest in search of fire for the hearth and encounters the fearsome and wise Baba Yaga. In Mesopotamian mythology, the goddess Inanna descends into the underworld and meets her sister Ereshkigal. Similarly, when we arrive at a place where our own path is intersected, we often come face-to-face with our own shadow selves.

At the crossroads our deepest fears and hidden wounds are illuminated, and some of our life's greatest teachers show up to give us the talisman, ask the right question, or to set us seemingly impossible tasks—impelling us to call upon a well of courage that we didn't even know we possessed. Astrology teaches us that there are definitive ages that coincide with distinct crossroads, and while there are similarities, everyone arrives at these thresholds with the specifics of their own lives and engages with the archetypes in a unique way. We each get the medicine that we require. However, it is also at these junctures where the real magic in our lives happens, where we are invited to take our place as the heroine or hero of our own story. This transitional space invites us into a state of becoming, as we enter the realm of possibility, soul crafting, and magic making.

Chances are if you are reading this book, you are either approaching a crossroads, in the middle of one, or trying to make sense of one that you've just gone through. If this is you, take heart. Learning about where you're at and the underlying developmental purpose of why you're there can bring clarity, comfort, and meaning. The archetypal dimensions of your own story become illuminated. You realize that you have entered the transpersonal realm where healing, magic, and alchemy can occur. Knowing just where you are on the path can be a lantern in the dark.

Temenos is a concept used by Swiss psychologist C. G. Jung denoting a place of refuge, a place of protection and sanctuary where one can find the solace needed to do their inner work. When people come to me for counsel, my intention is to create just such a container—a time outside of time—to hold space for those who enter. That is my intention with this book.

So, I invite you across the threshold of my cottage door and bid you sit at my table. Whatever crossroads you find yourself at, I have something for you.

Introduction

Who among us has not experienced a dark night of the soul? Who has not found themselves standing at a crossroads, not knowing how to proceed? Perhaps you are there now as you read these words, and finding your way to this book has not been by mere chance but by some fortuitous moment of serendipity.

I wrote this book as an alternative way of gaining insight during the difficult passages of life. All too often, when we find ourselves in a dark night of the soul, or at a crossroads, the conventional ways of understanding the deeper aspects of where we are can fall short of the mark. Intuitively, we know we need something more, something that speaks to us at a soul level. We long to drop down and uncover the layers of meaning beneath the surface events that unfold in our lives. Just on the edge of our awareness, we intuit correctly that we are the protagonists of our own sacred story and that these junctures along the path are all somehow part of our unfolding personal myth—our heroic journey. We intuitively sense that there is a deeper meaning to these times. I have found that sacred astrology can be a useful complement to therapy and self-help, and it can illuminate the path in a way that brings the underlying archetypal meaning of a given rite of passage to light.

In this book you will find out when to expect the crossroads times throughout your life so you can make peace with the past, navigate the present, and create a more purposeful future. As you gain an understanding of the underlying purpose of where you're at, you'll discover the keys to increased self-realization and step into alignment with who you're becoming. You will be empowered to reclaim a sense of authenticity as you move toward your unique purpose. As you work through the rituals and guided meditations, you will discover how sacred astrology can help you in a practical way as you decipher the lessons the universe is trying to teach you and get clear about what you're calling in.

In this book you will discover how myth, folklore, and story can be a source of guidance in challenging times. You will learn how to create a self-care plan that addresses the distinct issues that can come up with the crossroad you're currently navigating. You will also have the opportunity to unlock new levels of self-awareness through ritual and guided meditation crafted specifically for each threshold. Further, as you learn about the various rites of passage, you'll be able to support family, friends, and coworkers who are going through difficult times with a better understanding of where they're at and what they're going through. For those in the helping professions, having some knowledge of these psycho-spiritual thresholds and the ages at which they occur can bring useful transpersonal insight when working with clients. And while sacred astrology is not a substitute for mental health care, it can be a beneficial complement to both therapy and self-help.

Re-enchant Your Life:
Finding Meaning through Story

Whether we realize it or not, throughout our lives, we play out the same stories that come down to us from mythology, folklore, and fairy tale. Contemplating the hidden wisdom found in story can provide guidance when we find ourselves in a dark wood. The motif of the dark wood is found throughout literature, fairy tale, and Jungian psychology and usually signifies a rite of passage, a time outside of time when the protagonist must make their way through a liminal place of uncertainty before they arrive at a new state of consciousness. The dark wood is a wild and unpredictable place, outside the bounds of the protagonist's known world, and usually filled with a sense of both enchantment and danger. Swiss literary theorist and author Max Lüthi explains that "every important turning point in development, every transition from one stage of life to another, is felt as a threat."[1] One can find oneself in the dark wood by many different paths: a breakup, illness, divorce, grief, the loss of a cherished job, the loss of faith—the ways into the forest are many.

In the widely known fourteenth-century narrative poem *The Divine Comedy*, Dante wrote, "Midway upon the journey of our life / I found myself in a forest dark, / For the straightforward pathway had been lost." The poem continues with the lines, "I cannot well repeat how there I entered, / So full was I with slumber at the moment / In which I had abandoned the true way."[2] These words, written over 700 years ago, resonate just as clearly in our contemporary lives as they did when Dante wrote them: losing our way, and not knowing how we got there, because we were asleep and lost our connection to our vital sense of purpose. Of course, Dante is referring to the loss of his religious faith, but archetypally it amounts to the same: the loss of a guiding principle, connection, and meaning.

The dark wood is also a recurring theme in fairy tale and folklore. Professor and author Theodora Goss writes, "The heroine never dies in the dark forest. Seriously, never. When you're in the dark forest, you're afraid. You feel as though it might be the end of the story: you might be lost forever. But it's never the end of the story, and that's another thing that fairy tales teach us. The dark forest is where you're lost and afraid, but it's not where you die. It's only a part of the journey, not the whole of it. The dark forest has one power over

---

1. Max Lüthi, *Once Upon a Time: On the Nature of Fairy Tales* (Bloomington: Indiana University Press, 1976), 24.
2. Dante Alighieri, *The Divine Comedy*, vol. 1, trans. Henry Wadsworth Longfellow (Boston: Fields, Osgood & Co., 1871), canto 1, lines 1–3, 10–12.

you, which is the power to frighten you. But that's it. And that realization can help you keep going."[3]

Through story, we can reframe the past and gain an understanding of the archetypal energetics beneath the circumstances of our lives. Story provides the key that unlocks the transpersonal realm where healing, magic, and transformation can occur. Author Terri Windling writes, "The safe return from the jungle, the forest, the spirit world, or the land of death often marks, in traditional tales, a time of new beginnings: new marriage, new life, and a new season of plenty and prosperity enriched not only by earthly treasures but those carried back from the Netherworld."[4]

So, we see that time spent in the dark wood is an important and necessary step in our individuation. And the crossroad transits are often when we find ourselves in that shadowy, uncertain terrain. No matter how dark the forest, it's important to take heart and keep faith that even this is part of our path. We need to be patient with ourselves and trust the process. There is no rushing initiation, and the gifts that come from our time in the dark wood will reveal themselves when we finally emerge. Going through the dark wood is precisely how the protagonist becomes the hero. Sometimes we feel guilt or shame when we've strayed unwittingly into the dark forest. We may feel we are not doing enough, that we should somehow snap out of it, pick ourselves up, and get on with things. Society shames us for taking time out, chides us for not being busy enough or not accomplishing enough in the topside world. For not "crushing" our goals fast enough. Perhaps we fear we'll be left behind if we don't keep up at breakneck speed and will never catch up to those whose Instagram accounts show us a carefully curated version of the perfect industrious life. But the truth is time runs differently in the dark forest. It is a

---

3. Theodora Goss, "Heroine's Journey," *Theodora Goss* (blog), December 17, 2014, https://theodoragoss.com/2014/12/17/heroines-journey-the-dark-forest/.

4. Terry Windling, "On Illness: In a Dark Wood," *Myth & Moor* (blog), October 17, 2019, https://www.terriwindling.com/blog/2019/10/on-illness-in-a-dark-wood.html.

rare opportunity to lean into the liminal, to drop down and align with our own becoming. If we make our way one step at a time and remain receptive, we will receive the guidance and inspiration we need. We will return wiser than before, with deeper self-knowledge and new insights to share.

Each crossroads transit is a significant chapter in the bigger picture of your whole life story, and as such, these times are the perfect opportunity for a life review. Each of us is the protagonist, the hero of our own story. Exploring your story through writing can give you an overview of your life that can be cathartic and healing and provide rich symbolic meaning to events in your past. It can also guide you toward your next steps. Take a moment to reflect on your own story. Are there recurring patterns or motifs that emerge?

Acknowledging our own narratives can be a radical act and one of our most worthwhile tasks. When we do so, we see that there is magic and wisdom woven into the warp and the weft of our journey. All stories are teaching tales, and whether we take the time to reflect on our own stories or share them with loved ones and community, they can help us connect to a deeper sense of meaning. Story shapes our perceptions and worldview. Throughout our lives, we all experience our own calls to adventure, rites of passage and initiations, and through the retelling of our stories, we can provide a light in the dark for others in these challenging times. It's particularly important for women, people of color, and the LGBTQ+ community to tell their stories. Throughout history, these voices have been silenced, ignored, or forgotten. Reclaiming and honoring all our stories inspires resistance and courage and can show us the lay of the land when we are at a crossroads.

Carl Jung wrote, "I took it upon myself to get to know 'my' myth, and I regarded this as the task of tasks."[5] What is *your* personal myth? What archetypal themes are you playing out in your life? From

---

5. C. G. Jung, *Symbols and Transformation*, vol. 5 of *Collected Works of C. G. Jung* (Princeton, NJ: Princeton University Press, 2014), xxv.

"Vasilisa the Beautiful" to the descent of the goddess Inanna, we see that the protagonist always undergoes a time in the metaphorical dark wood that reveals their true power and wisdom. Viewing our own stories from a mythological perspective is not only empowering; it can be life-changing.

What stories do you tell yourself about your life? Perhaps the right question is *how* do you tell yourself your life's stories? What words do you use? What feelings do they evoke? Re-framing your story can be profoundly cathartic and deeply healing. This is not about making up things that didn't happen or negating important things that did. It's about choosing to view your story through a new and empowering perspective. It's about the alchemical process of transforming lead into gold: turning the challenges of your life into your own unique strengths and hard-won wisdom. Brené Brown writes, "When we deny our stories, they define us. When we own our stories, we get to write a brave new ending."[6] If you are at a crossroads, taking some time to reflect on your life's path up to this point can give you a new sense of wholeness and context.

My Story in a Nutshell

Since I am encouraging you to reframe your story through an archetypal perspective, I've decided to share some of my own story with you. I have struggled for many years to tell my story publicly, as only a handful of my closest friends have ever been privy to it. By necessity, this tale must begin with my father, a complicated man plagued by his own personal demons. My father suffered some of the most shocking examples of child abuse imaginable, which left him with deep emotional scars, and unfortunately came of age in a time when mental health issues carried a stigma and seeking help was often seen as a sign of weakness. The only solace from his restless ghosts was

---

6. Brené Brown, "Own Our History. Change the Story," *Brené Brown* (blog), June 18, 2015, https://brenebrown.com/blog/2015/06/18/own-our-history -change-the-story/.

to be found at the bottom of a whiskey bottle, which meant my own childhood was set against the backdrop of substance misuse, unbridled rage, misogyny, shame, and unchecked mental health issues.

Books were my only escape, but even then it was not uncommon for my father to barge into my room without warning, destroying my stolen moments of peace with his narcissistic bids for attention. Many of my childhood friends were forbidden to spend time at my house once their parents learned of my father's issues. Therefore, I spent much of my childhood reading, writing stories, and drawing in my room. Mine was often a lonely childhood, and self-worth was hard to come by. Before I even had words for it, I was given to mysticism and, beginning in fourth grade, found solace and meaning in books on comparative religion, mythology, and folklore. In my first book, *The Twelve Faces of the Goddess*, I describe the life-changing moment when I happened upon a copy of Waite's *The Pictorial Key to the Tarot* in a free book bin in the school library. I took it home, taking care to keep it safely hidden, and cut the images out of the book, thus creating my very first tarot deck. This was my first real step into the esoteric, and it opened my eyes to a world of magic I did not know existed until then.

By the time I was 17, things at home had reached a breaking point, and I feared for not only my own mental health but at times my safety. I didn't know where I would go or what I would do, but I knew I would have to act on my own behalf if I was to survive. On a dark rainy November morning, instead of going to school, I packed a few belongings into a bag, walked down to the highway, and stuck out my thumb. Before I knew it, I had left my island village behind and crossed the water, finding myself caught in the bewildering lights of the city, with fifteen dollars in my pocket. Before I could get my bearings, Hades had dragged me down into the underworld, both figuratively and literally, and it would be some time before I resurfaced.

Time passed, and after extricating myself from a marriage that perhaps unsurprisingly echoed many of the themes from my childhood, I found myself raising my young son on my own. During my Saturn return, I had the opportunity to work in London, and on a break, I made my first pilgrimage to Glastonbury. The magic and healing I found there were the medicine I needed to slowly find my way back to myself. However, it would still be some time before I could leave the underworld entirely, because it was there that I made my livelihood. But the seeds had been planted, and I delved even deeper into my spiritual studies, including astrology. I did charts for friends, but it would be some time before I could make a full-time living as an astrologer. I wanted more than anything to leave behind the cage I'd been in since I was 17, and to give my son a better life, but with no education and nothing I could put on a résumé, I could not yet see my path out.

One night, unable to sleep because of an excruciating toothache, I made my way downstairs to my bookshelf and picked up the first book my hand landed on. It was Dr. Clarissa Pinkola Estés's *Women Who Run with the Wolves*. The book had sat on my shelf for years, but every time I went to read it, it didn't seem to be the right time. But that night, I began reading where it fell open, and I read until sunrise. All the answers to my questions had fallen into place, and I vibrated with a renewed sense of purpose and destiny. By morning I knew beyond any shadow of doubt that my task was to distill all that I had learned in the shadow realm so I could help other women who were struggling to reclaim their power. It was as if my path was illuminated and laid out before me, and while I knew it would be a long, hard road, I knew exactly what steps I needed to take.

Without delay, I completed the high school equivalency tests, applied for a student loan, and soon after enrolled in university to study psychology and gender studies. Study came surprisingly easy to me, considering I had quit school in the eleventh grade, and I excelled with a consistent 4.0 GPA. After reading my papers, psychology of gender professors routinely deferred to me as a subject matter expert, and I applied for and won several awards and scholarships. However, going to school without financial support and raising a child on my own was far from easy, and there were times when I thought my time in purgatory would never end. The sacrifices were many, and there were interruptions along the way, but quitting was not an option. I knew intuitively that this was part of the path and that I could not help anyone else until I had undergone this road of trials and made it to the other side. When I finally graduated with distinction, it was one of the most profound and hard-earned thresholds I had ever crossed.

Sometimes the path the gods have us walk is full of twists and turns that we don't understand until after the passage of time, but I have finally come to a place of gratitude and self-compassion for my unconventional lifepath. It has given me an uncommon perspective and hard-won wisdom that I would not have acquired any other way, as I learned firsthand about the toxic masculine and the gendered nature of power, and in a place that resembled a tavern more than a temple, I discovered the sacred where one might least expect to find it. I learned about sisterhood, belonging, the healing power of sacred sensuality on one's own terms, and the meaning of resilience. And, perhaps most importantly, I learned what it means to reclaim sovereignty after it has been stolen.

What Is Sacred Astrology?

Astrology is a symbolic language of energy, as I wrote in my book *The Twelve Faces of the Goddess,* and when we come to see how its patterns are aligned with changing seasons of the earth, it becomes an evocative language that aligns us with the immanent divinity in nature and our own deeper selves.

Sacred astrology is a spiritual path. If this statement comes as a surprise to you, you're not alone. In fact, even pairing the words *sacred* and *astrology* together may seem like a stretch in a culture that has largely forgotten astrology's ancient roots. Mercury retrograde hype and Sun sign columns skim the surface (at best), and yet many have been led to believe that this is the extent of astrology. When people tell me they don't "believe" in astrology, I forgive them, because the superficial brand of astrology that permeates much of popular culture is indeed hard to swallow for someone who is also a critical thinker. I don't believe in that kind of astrology either. And I certainly don't equate the average online Sun sign column with the sacred. But let's dig a little deeper.

The most ancient form of astrology was rooted in the movement of the sun and moon. The ancestors would have looked up at the night sky and observed that the cycles of women's fertility corresponded with the changing faces of the moon. Not having the convenience of artificial light, they would have tracked the phases of the moon and marked important feast days and celebrations when the light of the full moon illuminated the darkness. In time, they would have noticed that the cycles of growing things also corresponded with the phases of the moon and would plant and harvest their crops accordingly. Early people who made their living by the sea would have noted the correlation between the moon's phases and the tides and the subsequent effect on their catch. Author Sharynne MacLeod NicMhacha writes, "Because of its brilliance, its ability to transform itself, its perceived beneficence and assistance with important earthly considerations, concepts of great spiritual significance became associated with the moon, and its remarkable transformations. Hence, the moon was often regarded as the abode of a deity or thought of as a deity in and of itself."[7]

Underlining the importance of the moon in the lives of early peoples, the oldest known lunar calendar in the world is estimated to have been built around 8000 BCE at Warren Field in Aberdeenshire, Scotland. Predating Mesopotamian calendars by around 5,000 years (which were thought to be the oldest calendars in the world prior to the excavation of the calendar at Warren Field in 2004), the calendar is also noteworthy because it was believed to have been built by hunter-gatherers for predicting the movement of game, rather than by early farmers who were known for building monumental structures.

---

7. Sharynne MacLeod NicMhacha, *Queen of the Night: Rediscovering the Celtic Moon Goddess* (York Beach, ME: Red Wheel/Weiser, 2005), 7.

The lunar calendar is also aligned with the winter solstice to mark the changing of the seasons.[8] Another example of the moon's significance in ancient civilizations can be found at the Lascaux caves in central France. Some researchers believe that the nearly 15,000-year-old images include a lunar map that depicts the phases of the moon.[9]

Given humankind's propensity for meaning-making, it is easy to surmise how the moon's changing face became symbolic for early humans, connected to such concepts as the cyclical nature of life: birth, death, and rebirth. Over time, through the observation of patterns connected to the moon's fluctuating appearance, eclipses and other moon-related phenomena came to be interpreted as portents that foreshadowed events. Cross-culturally, since the earliest times, humankind's natural inclination for storytelling has layered the moon with myth and magic, associating it with numerous deities, spiritual significance, and myriad tales. And at its secret heart, what is astrology but a compendium of the countless stories that compose the mystery of life?

The sun too has played an important role in the earliest incarnations of astrology. Newgrange, in the Boyne Valley of County Meath, Ireland, is a 5,200-year-old passage tomb that is known widely for the illumination of its passage and chamber by the winter solstice sunrise. Older than Stonehenge and the Great Pyramids, Newgrange is a sacred site steeped in mystery. The site Newgrange.com states that although Newgrange is classified as a passage tomb, it is of significantly more import, and "Ancient Temple is a more fitting classification, a place of astrological, spiritual, religious and ceremonial importance, much as present day cathedrals are places of prestige and worship where

---

8. BBC News, "'World's Oldest Calendar' Discovered in Scottish Field," July 15, 2013, https://www.bbc.com/news/uk-scotland-north-east -orkney-shetland-23286928.
9. BBC News, "Oldest Lunar Calendar Identified," October 16, 2000, http:// news.bbc.co.uk/2/hi/science/nature/975360.stm.

dignitaries may be laid to rest."[10] I had the honor of visiting New-grange in September 2019. Entering this ancient temple was truly one of the most numinous experiences in all my travels. The passage is so narrow that visitors are not permitted to enter the tomb with anything on the body, such as a bulky bag, backpack, or purse. The tunnel is dimly lit and winding, and you must be able to twist, bend, turn sideways, and lower your head in places. Entering Newgrange is not for those who suffer from claustrophobia, and I must confess that I occasionally fought down a rising sense of panic as I made my way into the center of this 5,000-year-old temple. In the womb-like chamber, the roof rises and a soft glow illuminates engraved megalithic art, including the evocative triple spiral. There is a hushed silence and the feeling of being in *temenos,* a safe enclosed sanctuary. It is not hard to imagine the reverence the ancestors had for this place as they waited in darkness for the rebirth of the sun at winter solstice, signifying a new year and the assurance that life would continue.

Across the Irish Sea, in Wiltshire, England, another iconic Neolithic monument has kept track of the summer and winter solstices for at least five thousand years. And although the early cultures that built Stonehenge left no written records and the purpose of the monument is the subject of much conjecture, we do know that at the summer solstice the sun rises dramatically behind the Heel Stone to illuminate the center of the stone circle. Conversely, at the winter solstice, the sun aligns with the Heel Stone at sunset, marking the return of the sun and lengthening days. Hundreds of human burial remains have been found around the site, and recent research shows that Stonehenge was mainly used in winter, as archaeological evidence has been found that determines the recurrence of massive midwinter feasts.[11] All of this suggests that despite whatever other

---

10. Boyne Valley Tours, "Newgrange.com," accessed November 18, 2020, https://www.newgrange.com/.

11. Maev Kennedy, "Stonehenge Bones May Be Evidence of Winter Solstice Feasts," *Guardian,* December 20, 2009, https://www.theguardian.com /culture/2009/dec/20/stonehenge-animal-bones-solstice-feast.

purposes it served, Stonehenge was built with astronomical and, quite likely, spiritual or ceremonial significance.

Another sacred site connected with the sun's yearly movement is the ancient Mayan site of Chichén Itzá in Mexico. There, the pyramid El Castillo displays a twice-yearly phenomenon aligned with the equinoxes. As the sun sets, its last rays cast a shadow down the ninety-one steps of the pyramid creating the image of a sinuous snake. Built between 750 and 1200 CE, Chichén Itzá is a sacred site of ceremonial significance that provides a glimpse into Mayan and Toltec cosmology. It is interesting to note that the astronomy of Chichén Itzá was so progressive for its time that it had the ability to predict solar eclipses.[12]

At its core, astrology is essentially the correlation between observations in the cosmos and events on Earth, which recalls the aphorism "as above, so below." Nicholas Campion, respected author and associate professor at University of Wales Trinity Saint David, writes, "There is no human society that does not somehow, in some way, relate its fears, concerns, hopes, and wishes to the sky, and to the organizing principle behind it, the cosmos. Neither is there any society that does not express at least some fascination with the sky and its mysteries."[13] The roots of Western astrology originate some 4,000 years ago in ancient Mesopotamia. From there it expanded into ancient Greece, Rome, the Islamic world, and finally Europe. Humans have derived spiritual meaning through the study of the sky for thousands of years and throughout myriad cultures and places, including China, southeast Asia, India, Egypt, and South America. If you would like to dig deeper into the history of astrology, I highly recommend the works of Campion, including his excellent source *Astrology and Cosmology in the World's Religions*.

At its heart, sacred astrology is spirit expressing itself through archetype and story. It is an approach to understanding the underly-

---

12. *National Geographic*, "Chichén Itzá," November 15, 2010, https://www
.nationalgeographic.com/travel/world-heritage/article/chichen-itza.

13. Nicholas Campion, *Astrology and Cosmology in the World's Religions* (New York: New York University Press, 2012), 1.

17

ing energetic principles of the universe as well as a path to self-knowledge. The twelve signs that make up astrology are the core archetypes that encompass all aspects of life. There is nothing you can think of that is not reflected in one or a combination of these foundational archetypes. As a symbolic language, astrology is a mirror of life in all its complexity. Sacred astrology does not connect to a specific deity or even a pantheon but embodies the energetic signature of all gods and goddesses across all time and cultures.

The twelve signs, or archetypes, correspond with the phases of the spiritual journey of the soul, beginning with the first sign, Aries, at the spring equinox and culminating with the last sign, Pisces. The spring equinox marks the beginning of the Sun's path through the zodiac, and Aries represents the individuated life force that emerges out of the collective. Aries is the beginning of the soul's individuation at the beginning of its spiritual sojourn through the twelve signs. Through a reincarnation or evolutionary perspective, by the time the soul has made the journey from Aries to Pisces, it has experienced the lessons inherent in each sign. Last sign Pisces is aligned with one of the holiest of Mysteries: the assurance of rebirth embodied in all endings. The zodiac is a circle, and sacred astrology teaches us that the nature of life is cyclical. Using the metaphor of Joseph Campbell's hero's journey, the soul begins its journey at the spring equinox with Aries (the call to adventure) and completes the cycle with Pisces (crossing of the return threshold) to be reborn again with Aries and the coming of spring. The crossroad transits illustrated in this book are important evolutionary chapters in your own sacred story in this lifetime, and the themes and lessons of each are connected to the unfolding journey of your higher self.

Although astrology is a many-layered and complex language, I have found that the most intuitive way to understand it is in connection with the changing seasons and the Wheel of the Year. Because astrology originated in the Northern Hemisphere, the archetypal resonance of the signs aligns with the seasonal shifts of that part of the world. For example, first sign Aries marks the spring equinox and the birth

of spring. In the Northern Hemisphere, spring is a time of new beginnings and the return of life after winter. Sap rises in the trees, buds
burst open to greet the sun, and birds begin to sing again in search
of a mate. If we reflect on the natural world during this time of year,
we get an understanding of the essence of the sign Aries. Aries is
known to be a self-starter. An initiator. A survivor. A warrior. And
so it follows throughout each of the twelve signs: the qualities of a
given archetype are closely woven with the character of the season
in which it occurs. If you would like to learn more about astrology's
correspondence with the seasons and the Wheel of the Year, as well
as the hero's journey and its connection to astrology, I have written
about these more in depth in my book *The Twelve Faces of the Goddess*.

Chapter 1

How to Work with This Book

While having some basic astrology knowledge can be an asset, the wonderful thing about working with this book is that you don't need to know anything other than your age. That being said, we are constantly having other transits to our charts all the time, so if any of these themes resonate with you now, please work with that part of the book regardless of whether you are currently in that life stage or not. Also, please note that the crossroads transits build and wane, and you could well be experiencing the themes of these significant junctures leading up to and away from those ages.

My intent is that any guidance or inspiration to be found in this book is accessible to all seekers, not just those versed in the vast subject of astrology. For those of you who are unfamiliar with the language of astrology, your birth chart is a snapshot of the heavens taken at the moment that you came into the world and took your first breath. It is as unique to you as your fingerprint, and no one has ever had the same chart as you in all of history, and no one ever will again. The birth chart has been called a psychic blueprint, or the map of one's soul. It reflects the core issues you've come here to work out, the gifts you are here to cultivate, and points to the essence of your life purpose. Essentially, your birth chart is a description of the interplay of energies that make you the unique being that you are—your energetic signature. Having your chart done by a professional astrologer or embarking on a study of your own chart can yield a wealth of powerful insight and self-knowledge.

While your birth chart stays the same, reflecting the qualities of the moment in time relative to the place in which you were born, the planets in our solar system keep moving. A *transit* is essentially when a planet moving through the heavens makes contact by degree and angle to a planet in your birth chart. When this happens, we get an idea of an upcoming energy cycle on your horizon by looking at the archetypes associated with each planet, as well as the aspect that is being made between those planets. Some aspects are easy, flowing, and constructive, such as the *trine* or *sextile*, while others can suggest potential conflict or the need to integrate the two energies, such as the *square* or *opposition*.

Some transits indicate a time of opportunity, flow, growth and abundance in your life, while others suggest important life lessons, a major developmental shift, or a crossroads. Transits have been used since ancient times by astrologers to forecast or predict unfolding motifs both in the collective and in a person's life. Having insight into *what time it is* in your life can be immensely useful. It's like having a guidebook or a map that lets you know what themes to expect and when. You can then engage more consciously with the energy at play, rather than react to it. Although it is not the intention of this book to describe astrology basics or all transits in detail, if you're called to delve deeper into these fascinating subjects, I suggest Steven Forrest's *Inner Sky* and *Changing Sky* as excellent starting points.

Each of the significant transits we will be discussing has a powerful purpose to help us move forward on our soul's journey in this lifetime. They teach us the lessons we came here to learn and nudge us onto the path we're meant to be on. As such, each of these portals is an initiation in the truest sense of the word. And although we experience countless transits throughout our lives, there are several that are game changers, and those are the ones we'll be diving into here. I have chosen to focus on the phase of life between the first and second Saturn returns: beginning with the first Saturn return that occurs in one's late 20s/early 30s, moving through the *Midlife Transits* that occur approximately between age 36 and 48, and concluding with the second Saturn return that occurs in one's late 50s. The first Saturn return coincides with stepping into self-realized authenticity, while the second Saturn return signifies moving into the phase of wisdom. The years in between these two major turning points are woven with the threads of creating a life: forging an identity, establishing a career, commitment or marriage, deciding whether or not to have children, working at mastering something of importance, making a unique contribution, facing life's many trials, the wakeup call of midlife, and, if we're receptive, finding magic and meaning along the way.

The years between these two significant thresholds define who we are as self-actualized adults. The transits we'll be discussing are known as *bio-psychic*, meaning they occur at approximately the same age for everyone, and they signify the steps we must take to awaken to our unique purpose. And while these thresholds often initially show up as a psychospiritual crisis characterized by challenge, confusion, or restlessness, they almost always coincide with the most significant turning points in our lives. They are significant rites of passage that can signify new levels of self-discovery and personal growth.

These rites of passage include the following:

The First Saturn Return: Age 27–30
The Midlife Transits

- Pluto Square: Age 36–48
- Neptune Square: Age 39–42
- Uranus Opposition: Age: 41–45
- Saturn Opposition: Age: 44–45

The Second Saturn Return: Age 58–60

Although these are the approximate average ages when these transits will occur, it's important to remember that we can start to experience the themes of these major transits a year or two before and then another year or two after the exact dates. This is because the energy of a major transit doesn't simply begin or end on a specific date, but it slowly builds and then wanes as the planet in question usually stays within *orb* of that degree for some time (within approximately 5 degrees).

Please also note that transits to Pluto, Neptune, and Uranus last approximately 1.5 years once they begin, so even though, for example, the average age for the Uranus opposition is somewhere between 41 and 45, it does not mean you will experience that transit for four years. If you would like to know the exact dates of your transits, there are various transit apps available, such as Time Passages and Time Nomad. However, for a deep dive into one of these pivotal turning points, consider booking a consultation with a professional astrologer, who can give you a comprehensive overview of not only the specific transit you're moving through, but how its lessons fit into your overall lifepath.

The planets in astrology are an energetic shorthand for a wealth of symbolic meaning, just as a word is a symbol for the meaning of a concept that we wish to convey. Let's take Saturn for example. If you understand the layers of meaning behind what we call Saturn, it will start to make more sense to you when you discover you're about to have your Saturn return. Astrology is a symbolic language of energy, and the planets are part of the vocabulary of that language. We could use other words for the same concepts, but those same concepts and archetypes exist no matter what you call them. Instead of naming it "the Saturn return," we could say this is a time in the human life cycle when a particular set of themes will arise, which may include a serious reality check, limitation, restriction, isolation, life review, and commitment to something important. But it's infinitely more convenient to learn something of the language, so someone can say "Saturn," and immediately you will have an idea of the meaning behind what that word or planet stands for. The archetype we call Saturn still exists if you were to give that set of meanings a different name. The planets are named after the Romanized versions of the Greek gods who embody an archetypal set of qualities that connect to a particular principle in life.

You can work with this book in several different ways. If you are currently within the age range of one of these significant transits, you can go directly to that chapter to understand where you're at. Be sure to make space to do the ritual, guided meditation, and the writing reflections to get a clear understanding of the threshold you're currently crossing. Simply reading the text will certainly give you some insight, but to move more consciously through the initiation of a given transit, you must be willing to do the work.

If you are at any age past your first Saturn return, you can also look up any of the transits you've already undergone to shed light on the past and gain clarity and insight on events or situations that may still trouble you. In my practice, I will often ask clients what was happening in their lives during previous transits. For example, I'll ask what was unfolding when they were between the ages of 27 and 30 (their first Saturn return). Most nod knowingly and respond immediately with answers such as "It was one of the most difficult and lonely times in my life, but I wouldn't be where I am now if those things didn't happen." Almost all say that they feel like a different person than they were before a significant transit. However, there are some who are still carrying grief and bewilderment from past events. They may have experienced real trauma in some way during their time at the crossroads and are still in the process of healing and recovery. Learning about a given time in your life and the purpose beneath your past experiences can provide retrospective clarity and deeper layers of meaning so you can heal and move on.

Alternatively, you can also look ahead to your next crossroads transit and reflect on the archetypal themes that will soon be emerging in your life. How can you prepare? Although we cannot predict exactly how a transit will play out according to the specifics in your life, an understanding of the motifs that will be activated can help you cocreate a more conscious experience. Understanding the archetypal patterns beneath the surface of your life can give you more control in the way they manifest in your outer world. For example, you may be in your mid-30s and realize that your Midlife Transits are not too far off on the horizon. Instead of just rushing headlong toward this pivotal turning point, distracted by the vagaries of daily life, you may choose to be proactive. Read about your next upcoming transit, get an understanding of the soon-to-emerge themes, and ask yourself some tough questions. What is important to you? What needs to change that you've been denying or procrastinating on? What relationships, career goals and patterns need to be reassessed? The more awake you can be to the evolutionary intent of an upcoming crossroad time, the more likely you will experience it as a profound opportunity for self-realization and personal growth.

Each part begins with a myth or folktale that aligns archetypally with the corresponding rite of passage. As you make your way through the chapter, reflect on the symbolic underpinnings of the story and how they may relate to your experience. You may wish to journal any insights that arise. Next, read about the planet that's associated with the transit. This will give you a clear picture of the themes you can expect to emerge. You are then ready to delve into the self-care tool-kit and align yourself with medicine that will help you navigate the passage with more ease and grace. Finally, each chapter concludes with correspondences to further enhance your journey, including deities, essential oils, stones and crystals, and plant allies.

Some Tools to Work with This Book

As you work your way through this book, here are a few notes to help you make the most of each section:

A Note on Therapeutic Ritual

Although it could be said that all ritual is potentially therapeutic in some way, the rituals in this book are designed to help you work with the kind of issues that can come up during the specific crossroad transits. The benefits of ritual and ceremony are becoming increasingly accepted and embraced as part of the therapeutic process by countless therapists. Ritual can facilitate the healing of old trauma and help shift one's narrative. It has also shown to be beneficial in treating anxiety. On the site Psychology Today, Dr. Nick Hobson states that "scholars have long known about the anxiolytic properties of rituals. They bring order and structure to a world that is inherently disordered and chaotic. Rituals are an effective shield that protect[s] us from the onslaught of uncertain events."[14] Ritual can mark important shifts in our lives and help us recognize our rites of passage. Ritual can help us manifest change, set new intentions, or release something that no longer serves us. It can be part of a new beginning and can bring closure. Ritual can help us acknowledge the important steps taken on our journey and bring profound symbolic meaning to important life transitions.

In her book *Braiding Sweetgrass*, Indigenous author and botanist Robin Klimmerer writes that ceremony "marries the mundane to the sacred. The water turns to wine, the coffee to a prayer. The material and the spiritual mingle like grounds mixed with humus, transformed like steam rising from a mug into the morning mist. What else can you offer the earth, which has everything? What else can you give but something of yourself? A homemade ceremony, ceremony that makes a home."[15] It is in transforming our experience at the crossroads into something sacred that we are given the chance to re-enchant our lives. To bring a sense of deep magic to our most difficult of trials so that they become meaningful chapters in our life story.

Most rituals include specific words, actions, and visualizations that enable us to focus our energy and connect with spirit, deity, or the personal subconscious. Some of you may already have your own way of

---

14. Nick Hobson, "The Anxiety-Busting Properties of Ritual," *Psychology Today*, September 25, 2017, https://www.psychologytoday.com/ca/blog/ritual -and-the-brain/201709/the-anxiety-busting-properties-ritual?collection =1108996.
15. Robin Wall Kimmerer, *Braiding Sweetgrass* (Minneapolis, MN: Milkweed Editions, 2014), 37–38.

preparing for ritual. Taking a few moments to clear the space you'll be working in, followed by grounding and centering, is beneficial before any kind of ritual. Depending on whether you follow a specific tradition, you may choose to cast a circle, call the quarters, or draw the compass round before engaging with ritual. Please follow your intuition and whatever path you are familiar with to prepare. It is my hope that the rituals I've included here will be adapted to the specifics of each reader, so that as many people as possible can benefit in the way that they need. If you are new to ritual and are interested in exploring it through a specific magickal tradition, there are countless books and educators from a variety of magickal traditions to learn from.

A Note on the Pathworkings

To get the most out of the guided pathworkings in this book, it is useful to first prepare your space. Minimize distractions by turning off your phone, dressing comfortably, and making sure you go to the bathroom before you begin. It can also be helpful to clear any clutter and straighten out your space beforehand. Be sure you have whatever you will need to be comfortable, such as a blanket, cushion, or supports. Before you begin, decide how you will experience the pathworking: you can read it, record yourself reading it on your phone and listen to the recording, or listen to an audio version of this book.

Light a candle and have a pen and your journal nearby to write down any messages or impressions that come up afterward. To deepen your experience, check the associated correspondences, and burn any (safe) herbs or essential oils of your choice that connect with the chapter you are working with. Alternatively, you may wish to burn protective herbs such as yarrow, hyssop, or mugwort before you begin. If you wish to facilitate lucid dreaming during or after the pathworking, consider taking mugwort (*Artemisia vulgaris*) tea approximately forty-five minutes before you begin. Mugwort tea is available in many natural food stores and online. Follow usage recommendations. Do not take mugwort if you are pregnant or think you might be pregnant, as it can bring on menstruation. Other herbs that can help you relax and ease into a receptive trancelike state include passionflower, wood betony, and skullcap. If you are unsure of the dosage, please consult an herbalist before taking any herb that you are unfamiliar with. Any of the pathworkings can be done with or without herbal support. If you do choose to use any of these herbs, make sure you do not have to drive or be anywhere for at least two hours after the pathworking.

Once you are comfortable and ready to begin, several square breaths will help you relax into a receptive state. Square breathing is a simple yogic breathing technique that is useful for calming, concentration, and focus. Breathe in for the count of four. Hold for the count of four. Breathe out for the count of four. Hold for the count of four, and repeat for a few cycles until you feel calm and centered.

After you are finished the pathworking, take some time to stretch and come back into the room. Drink a glass of water and be sure to record anything that came up in your journal. Watch your dreams for the next few nights, as your subconscious may still be processing deep internal material that will become clearer with reflection.

A Note on the Journal Reflections

When I book someone for a full natal soul chart session, I send out a new client form to help them prepare. And while this helps me focus on what's important for someone, it also prepares them on a subtle level for our work together. Asking a question can prompt a psychic shift that brings new insight. Journaling can be a form of meditation and one of the most cathartic things you can do for yourself during your crossroad transits. Journaling can help you get vague impressions and feelings out of your head and onto the paper, where they can give you a new perspective. A kind of magic happens once you make space to commit to a daily writing practice. As you connect with your inner Self, you may be surprised at the deep well of wisdom and guidance that comes through. Journaling can help you clarify your thoughts and understand your feelings. It can give you an overview of your life so you can make sense of the big picture. Shut off your inner critic and throw punctuation and spelling to the wind. You can write your reflections either in a notebook or on your computer. However, something interesting happens when you write longhand, as you access another part of your psyche that is hard to reach on a keyboard. Try it and see for yourself. Use the writing prompts in the chapter as a starting point but allow your writing to take its own direction. If you feel like writing longer than fifteen minutes, you know you're on to something. See where it takes you, and remember, no judgment! Journaling can be a powerful gateway to self-reflection that can show you the archetypal dimensions of your own story, as well as possible next steps.

A Note on Working Magickally with a Planet and Its Correspondences

Whether or not you are a magickal practitioner, it can be helpful to know something of the correspondences and allies associated with each planet. You could brew a tea with one of the (safe) herbs before doing a pathworking, carry one of the stones with you on a particularly stressful day or rough patch in your transit, burn an essential oil while journaling or preparing for ritual, or put a few drops into your bath. And you can meditate on the associated tarot card to align yourself with the themes of a given transit to gain deeper insight.

Part 1
A Lantern in the Dark

The dark night of the soul comes just before revelation.
When everything is lost, and all seems darkness, then comes
the new life and all that is needed.
Joseph Campbell

Chapter 2
Vasilisa the Beautiful

If there is any one tale that epitomizes the path through the dark wood, it is the Russian folktale "Vasilisa the Beautiful." And although there are many renditions of this story and it has been told in Russia and eastern Europe for countless generations, it may be old beyond reckoning.

I recommend that you read this story with intent, as though you were preparing for ritual. Find a place where you will not be disturbed, light a candle, and turn off your phone. Allow yourself to drop down into the tale and step between the worlds. This ancient tale is a rich source of guidance that can bring layers of insight at any crossroads, but its inherent wisdom is particularly relevant during the Saturn return, as we shall see.

Long ago, in a time outside of time, nestled somewhere east of the Carpathian Mountains, a mother lay on her deathbed. Her husband and young daughter, heads bent in sorrow, waited in silence while the clock on the mantel ticked away her final hours. A single candle flickered, and the scent of burning herbs filled the air. The mother raised her head just a little from her pillow and called her daughter to her side. "Vasilisa, it breaks my heart that I will not be here to watch you grow up. There are so many things I wanted to teach you, tales I wanted to give you, but my time in this world is not long. Listen carefully, for these are my last words." She reached beneath the woolen blanket and pulled out a little doll and handed it to Vasilisa. "If ever you are lost or do not know which way to turn, give her something to eat and ask her. Do not show her to anyone. Keep her secret and safe, and she will help you in your time of need. This is my blessing to you, my beautiful Vasilisa." Then, the mother's eyes closed, and she was still.

Vasilisa and her father mourned for a long time, as she was a good woman, and they felt her loss keenly. But as the wheel turned and winter gave way to the new green growth of spring, Vasilisa's father began to think of marrying again. A widow in a neighboring village caught his eye, and whether because of his loneliness or because he wanted his child to have a mother, he took her as his wife. The widow came with her two daughters to live with Vasilisa and her father. By all appearances, they were genteel and well-mannered ladies, but beneath the surface they were cold and conniving. Whenever the father went away on some business and Vasilisa was left alone with them, they forced her to gather firewood, light the stove, and do the hardest and most difficult tasks in the house. Eventually, Vasilisa had no life at all beyond toil, for the stepmother had conspired to marry Vasilisa's father not for love but because he was a wealthy merchant. And she had no use for Vasilisa, who had grown to be the most beautiful young woman in the village. Vasilisa was comely, with curves in all the right places and a radiant complexion like roses and cream. She was also kind, gracious, and gentle and did her work without complaint. In comparison, the stepsisters were ill favored and as spiteful as they were jealous. Every chance they got, they colluded to get Vasilisa to perform tasks that would mar her beautiful skin and detract from her beauty. But with each passing day, despite the relentless drudgery, Vasilisa became even more winsome.

As the years passed, Vasilisa reached the full blossom of womanhood, and young men rode out from neighboring villages to court her. Not one of them even gave the stepsisters a passing glance, which angered the stepmother, so she forbade that Vasilisa be married before her own daughters. Once the suitors were out of the house, she beat Vasilisa in her anger and frustration. The trio's jealousy and contempt for Vasilisa had come to a point where something needed to be done to rid themselves of her for once and for all. And so, they contrived a plan.

It came to pass that the merchant was called away on a lengthy journey to a distant land. As soon as he rode out of sight, the step-mother called her daughters to her side. "Girls, listen well, for the time has come. We will conspire for the fire to go out, and send Vasilisa off to get fire from Baba Yaga, the wild witch of the wood." The daughters squealed in delight at their mother's ingenuity. Hardly able to contain her glee, the eldest asked, "Does Baba Yaga not eat those who come to her door as if they were chickens?" The youngest inquired, "Does Baba Yaga not have iron teeth and use human bones as toothpicks?" The mother nodded, a slow, smug smile forming on her withered lips.

On a crisp autumn evening, Vasilisa returned from the forest where she had been gathering mushrooms to find the house almost in complete darkness, save for one candle sputtering in the window, which went out the moment she opened the door and crossed the threshold. The sisters shrieked, "All the fires have gone out, and now our last candle too! It is your fault, Vasilisa, for when you opened the door, you let in a gust of wind that extinguished our only light. You must go into the woods and bring fire from Baba Yaga so we may have light for cooking, you wicked girl!"

Vasilisa replied, "Yes, of course, we need light, and it is my fault the candle went out. I will go." She took a deep breath to steady herself, felt in her pocket to ensure the doll her mother gave her was there, and set out into the woods to seek Baba Yaga.

As she walked deeper into the forest, with only the ghostly light of a waning moon to find her way, she could scarcely see her feet as she made her way one step at a time along the path. Presently, she found herself standing at a crossroads. Vasilisa reached into her pocket and pulled out the doll, clutching it to her breast. "Which way do I go?" she whispered. The doll's eyes lit up like two stars, and Vasilisa took a little crust of bread from her pocket and gave it to the doll, who spoke: "Do not fear; as long as we are together, no harm shall come to you. Take the left path." And so Vasilisa continued deeper and deeper into the woods with the doll to guide her.

Suddenly, she heard the sound of galloping, and a man on horseback rode past her. The horse was as white as moonlight, and the rider dressed head to foot in white, and the forest became lighter with the breaking of dawn. On she walked. Sometime later, another man, dressed all in crimson, trotted by on a fiery red stallion, and as he passed her, the sun rose. Vasilisa walked the whole day, not knowing if she was any closer to Baba Yaga's hut, and was beginning to feel tired and quite hopeless. But as daylight began to fade, she came upon a clearing in the woods, and in the middle was a strange hut perched on chicken's legs, surrounded by a fence of bones topped with human skulls. The gate's hinges were made with the bones of human feet, and the locks were jawbones with sharp, pointed teeth. Vasilisa stopped in her tracks, her heart in her mouth. As she stood rooted to the spot in shock, a third man cantered past her, this time dressed all in black, astride an ebony horse. He rode out through the gate, and darkness fell. The eyes of the skulls lit up and cast an eerie glow over the clearing.

Suddenly, a great and terrible crashing, cracking, earsplitting cacophony echoed through the wood, and Baba Yaga appeared riding in a mortar, steering it with a pestle, and sweeping away her tracks with a birch broom. She landed before Vasilisa and roared, "What is it you seek?"

Vasilisa was paralyzed with fear, and she trembled as she replied, "Grandmother, all of the light in my house has gone out, and my stepsisters have sent me to ask you for fire."

The witch narrowed her eyes, and spoke, "Yes, I know who they are. If I give you the fire, you will need to stay for a while and work for me to earn it. If you do not—there will be consequences."

Vasilisa took in the spectacle of the fence of human bones and shuddered, "Yes, of course, Grandmother. I will work for you in exchange for the light."

With a wave of Baba Yaga's gnarled hand, the gate opened, and she rode in with Vasilisa behind her, as the gate shut fast behind them. In the hut, Baba Yaga laid herself upon her bed and yawned. "I have been working all day, gathering herbs and tending to what matters. I am hungry. Serve me what cooks in that pot." Vasilisa went quickly to the kitchen and ladled cabbage soup into a bowl. She got a loaf of bread from the oven, and went to the cellar and brought up kvass, mead, and elderflower wine. Baba Yaga ate it all and left but a crust of bread and small cup of soup for Vasilisa. "When I leave in the morning, I want you to clean the yard, sweep the house, make dinner, do the laundry, and go to the granary to separate the rotting grains from the good wheat. When I return, I will make sure you have done all your chores. If you don't—there will be consequences." The old woman then turned over, pulled the feather comforter up over her head, and went to sleep.

Vasilisa crept into a corner and took the little doll from her pocket. She shared some of her bread and soup with the doll and asked, "What am I to do? Baba Yaga has asked me to perform impossible tasks in so little time. If I don't, I fear what will become of me." The little doll's eyes lit up like fireflies. "Do not worry, Vasilisa. I am here, and I will help you. Be sure to eat something and get some rest. Morning is wiser than evening."

Early the next morning, Vasilisa looked out the window and saw Baba Yaga climbing into her mortar. It was still dark, but as she watched, the rider in white galloped out on his pale horse, leaped over the gate and into the forest, and it was dawn. Sometime after, the man dressed in crimson trotted around the hut and leaped over the gate on his fiery red steed, and the sun rose. With a start, she remembered all the work that needed to be done, but she looked out the window, and realized that the yard was tidy. Turning back to the room, she saw the floors were swept, and all was in order. Vasilisa let herself outside and went to the granary where the little doll was just finishing separating the rotten wheat from the good wheat.

The doll had taken care of all the chores that the Baba Yaga had laid out for Vasilisa. In gratitude, Vasilisa went back to the hut to rest and think about what she would prepare for Baba Yaga's evening meal. Alone in the hut, she stared around her in wonder at the abundance there. Jars of healing herbs neatly lined the shelves. The pantry was full to overflowing with provisions and the larder stocked. A soft sheepskin blanketed the floor, and the feather comforter on Baba Yaga's bed was richly embroidered with bright red poppies.

As darkness fell, Baba Yaga returned and could find no fault with Vasilisa's work. "Hmm, you have done well. Tomorrow, do it all again. And I have one other task for you. Go to the granary and clean all the dirt from the poppy seeds." Baba Yaga ate her evening meal and then climbed into her bed, pulled the comforter up over her head, and went to sleep. Vasilisa crept out to the granary and saw an enormous mountain of dirt mixed with poppy seeds, and her heart sank. She reached into her pocket, took out the little doll, and fed it a little that was left over from supper. The doll's eyes glowed like the sparks of a campfire. "Do not lose heart, Vasilisa. Eat something and get some sleep. Morning is wiser than evening."

The next morning Baba Yaga again rode off in her mortar, steering her way through the forest with the pestle, and sweeping away her tracks with the broom as she went. When she returned in the evening, just as the black rider had jumped over the gate, she demanded to see Vasilisa's work. Sure enough, the yard was tidy, the floors were freshly swept, supper was on the stove, and out in the granary, each poppy seed had been sorted from the dirt into two neat piles. Baba Yaga's eyes narrowed. "Hmm, you have done all I asked. Lay the table for supper." Vasilisa set the table and served Baba Yaga a sumptuous feast of borscht, potatoes with dill, and *pelmeni* slathered in butter. While the witch washed it all down with multiple cups of elderflower wine, mead, and rich, dark kvass, Vasilisa stood looking on.

Baba Yaga finished her supper, pushed her plate and cup out of the way, and folded her hands in her lap. "Is there something you wish to ask me?"

Vasilisa took a deep breath. "Yes, Grandmother, I do have some questions if that is all right."

"Go ahead, ask," rumbled Baba Yaga, "but remember, to know too much too soon can make one grow old before their time. What would you like to know?" Vasilisa asked about the man in white on the white horse.

Baba Yaga smiled, "Aha! That is my New Day."

"And what of the man dressed all in red on the fiery stallion?"

"That is my Beautiful Sun."

"And what is the meaning of the man all dressed in black on the steed black as jet?"

Baba Yaga smiled again, "That is my Deepest Night." She narrowed her eyes. "Would you like to ask me more questions, Granddaughter?"

Vasilisa thought for a moment, but her intuition warned her to be silent.

"No, Grandmother, as you said, too much knowledge too soon will make one grow old before their time."

Baba Yaga sat back, closed her eyes, and chuckled softly to herself. "Now it is my turn to ask you a question, my child. How have you managed to get all the tasks I have given you done in so little time?"

Vasilisa's stomach tightened, and a sweat broke out upon her forehead. She stammered, "My—my mother's blessing helps me."

"I knew it!" Baba Yaga got up, turning over the table. "Be on your way before there are consequences!" She grabbed Vasilisa by the elbow and pushed her outside and through the gate, where she took a skull with glowing eyes from off the fence and shoved it in her hands.

"There is your fire! There is your light! You have gotten what you came for. Take it back to your stepmother and stepsisters, and may they use it well!"

Vasilisa found a stick and stuck the skull on it, and she ran all through the night and into the next day until night fell again. She carried the burning skull as a lantern to illuminate her path until she finally reached the edge of the forest. Now that she was so close to home, she looked at the skull with its glowing eyes and went to throw it away, but the skull whispered to her, "You have earned the fire, Vasilisa. Take me to your stepmother." As she approached the house, she noticed it was all dark. When the stepmother and stepsisters saw Vasilisa returning home and bearing fire, they cried in relief, "Oh, thank goodness! Every time we have brought fire to the house to cook our food or to see by, it went out as soon as we crossed the threshold! Maybe the witches' fire will keep burning."

They brought the skull inside and gave it pride of place on a table in the center of the house. The skull glowed with ever more intensity, as its eyes followed the stepmother and stepsisters all through the night. In the morning, the three were burnt to ashes. As the sun rose, Vasilisa went outside and dug a deep hole beside an elder tree, where she buried the skull. She then locked the house with a key and set off toward the village.[16]

"Vasilisa the Beautiful" draws many parallels to the first Saturn return, and Baba Yaga is a Saturnian Teacher if ever there was one. She is the quintessential wise woman living alone in a cottage in the woods, and not only is she aligned with the Saturnian motifs of time, death, fear, and the cycles of life, she is also emblematic of the idea of consequences for avoiding the work. Many renditions of the story represent her in an almost cartoonish way: the frightening witch who eats the humans who arrive at her door with gnashing iron teeth, reminiscent of the mythological Saturn in his guise as "the Devourer."

---

16. Post Wheeler, *Russian Wonder Tales* (New York: Century Company, 1912), https://openlibrary.org/books/OL7236461M/Russian-wonder_tales; Clarissa Pinkola Estés, *Women Who Run with the Wolves* (New York: Ballantine, 1992), 75–80.

Many variations of the story include a passage where Baba Yaga throws Vasilisa out of her hut after she learns that she has her mother's blessing, with some variation of "Blessing! We need no blessings in this house!" My sense is that if the story is as old as some claim it to be, there is another version of Baba Yaga that may have existed before she was demonized as the "evil witch." I have decided to retell it from a more sympathetic, human perspective, while still remaining true to the foundation of the story.

I've always found it fascinating that Baba Yaga rides in a mortar, steered by a pestle. A mortar and pestle have long been one of the tools of the trade of the herbalist. Archetypally, a mortar and pestle align with transformation, transition, magic and the mysteries of plant medicine. It is a kind of cauldron, a container in which something is mixed, crushed, beaten, and alchemized into something new. To me, the mortar and pestle allude to a connection with Baba Yaga and herbs/plant medicine, suggesting she is not only a stern teacher but also a healer and a medicine woman. Baba Yaga is both wisewoman and Keeper of the Mysteries. In the book *Baba Yaga: The Wild Witch of the East in Russian Fairy Tales* Sibelan Forrester writes, "Given the strong possibility that she played a role in stories of initiation, it is no surprise that today Baba Yaga is used by Jungian therapists as a figure of dark, occult knowledge, and her hut to symbolize a stage on a difficult path."[17]

The tale is a coming-of-age story that begins with a deep and life-altering loss, a common theme during a major Saturn transit. The Saturn return marks a pivotal turning point for all who come to this threshold, and it is often a time of breaking away from parental influence, the beginning of forging one's own life based on one's own values regardless of how long one has actually been out of the nest. Whether the experience of the original home was a supportive one or more challenging, the Saturn return is the time to carve out our own

---

17. Sibelan Forrester, trans., *Baba Yaga: The Wild Witch of the East in Russian Fairy Tales*, ed. Sibelan Forrester, Helena Goscilo, and Martin Skoro (Jackson: University Press of Mississippi), xli.

separate identity. It is a time to "separate the seeds"—to ascertain family patterns of trauma and antiquated values and to witness the intersections of privilege and oppression that have been handed down. Paradoxically, it is also a time to learn discernment and to honor the wisdom of the elders. Astrologer and author Erin Sullivan writes that the Saturn return is a rebirth aspect "reminiscent of that initial separation from the mother and the first stages of independence. This is not always done gracefully; indeed, it can be as shocking as the birth moment...one looks at one's life from a new perspective."[18]

The loss or separation that precipitates that new perspective can come from many sources, besides a breaking away from family influences. We may lose a relationship, a job, our direction, or our sense of self. In the story, Vasilisa loses her mother, which, much like the Saturn return, represents a loss of comfort, safety, innocence, and identity. However, Vasilisa's mother leaves her with something—the little doll—to guide and protect her in times of uncertainty. While the doll symbolizes the innate wisdom that we all have within, it also represents handed-down ancestral wisdom, the ability to connect with those who have gone before for guidance. It is that wise inner voice who knows the next steps and can show us the way if only we listen. Author Clarissa Pinkola Estés conflates the doll with intuition, and explains that "talismans are reminders of what is felt but not seen, what is so, but is not immediately obvious. The talismanic numen of the image of the doll reminds us, tells us, sees ahead for us."[19] During the Saturn return, we are usually given ample opportunity to develop and trust our intuition.

Vasilisa is sent into the dark wood by her stepsisters to get fire. Symbolically, the fire element is connected to light, life force, wisdom, and transformation. It is also necessary for survival. In the time before electricity, fire was the only source of warmth and light. It was

---

18. Erin Sullivan, *Saturn in Transit: Boundaries of Mind, Body, and Soul* (New York: Penguin, 2005), 72.

19. Estés, *Women Who Run with the Wolves*, 91.

used for cooking, keeping predators away, and illuminating the darkness so one could see. Our protagonist sets off alone on this important mission—it is up to her and only her to bring back the light. During the Saturn return, it is common to feel alone and unaccompanied on our journey as we tend to the important task of individuation. This is often the first step of taking on more self-responsibility, an important Saturn theme. Vasilisa makes her way one step at a time through the dark forest, which is the only way forward during a significant Saturn transit. Perseverance despite fear of the unknown is the only way through.

Fear is a common thread throughout this tale, and Saturn is also thematically connected to fear. The saying "feel the fear and do it anyway" sums up a major Saturn time. Like Vasilisa, we often find ourselves trembling with fear of the unknown, fear of what's next, or fear of not being enough. Vasilisa feels fear as she makes her way through the dark wood, fear as she stands in the clearing and beholds the hut surrounded by human bones, and fear when she is asked to do an impossible set of tasks in precious little time. And this is certainly how it can feel during our Saturn return. Sometimes it feels as though we are confronted with one daunting challenge after another, with barely enough time to catch our breath. But this is the work. This is the way one becomes the hero of their own story. One step at a time.

Vasilisa finally arrives at her destination, and it is a sight to behold. A strange little hut perched on chicken's legs, surrounded by a fence made of human bones. Forrester writes, "She (Baba Yaga) mediates the boundary of death so that living human beings may cross it and return, alive but in possession of new wisdom, or 'reborn' into a new status."[20] Like fear, death is also a Saturn theme, and the Saturn return is often a time when we are faced with a realization of our own mortality. As people get closer to 30, many realize with a shock that they are not going to live forever. If one went through their early 20s with a devil-may-care attitude, this time can bring with it a sobering

---

20. Forrester, *Baba Yaga*, xxxiv.

realization that life is finite and precious. It can also bring an awareness that it's time to step up to the plate and get on track with what is truly important. Many are in fact reborn in a sense, acquiring new wisdom after undergoing Saturn's return. However, it is not only literal mortality that a Saturn transit relates to. Other endings that can feel like a death may show up, for it is the end of a phase of life, and before the next phase begins, we may feel betwixt and between, neither here nor there.

By the time Vasilisa has reached the hut, she has seen the white and red rider, and as she stands before the little house in the clearing, the black rider leaps over the gate and into the woods. As we read in the tale, these three riders represent dawn, the rising sun, and night, pointing to Baba Yaga's connection with the cycles of time. Estés writes, "The black, red, and white horsemen symbolize the ancient colors connoting birth, life, and death. These colors also represent old ideas of descent, death, and rebirth—the black for dissolving of one's own values, the red for the sacrifice of previously held illusions, and the white as the new light, the new knowing that comes from having experienced the first two."[21]

Before Baba Yaga agrees to let Vasilisa cross her threshold, she tells her yes, she will give her the light she seeks, but she will have to earn it, or there will be consequences. More Saturn parallels. Saturn is connected to hard work, but also to the idea of working to earn something of true value. Saturn is also aligned with the consequences that arise from the actions we take and do not take. Like Baba Yaga, Saturn provides just rewards for those willing to do the work.

On her first morning in Baba Yaga's hut, Vasilisa notices the abundance all around her in this unlikely place. Jars of herbs line the shelves, the larder is overflowing with food, a soft, warm sheepskin lies on the floor, and a beautiful feather blanket embroidered with poppies lies atop Baba Yaga's bed. This not only hints at the rich rewards bestowed on those who work in accordance with *what is*, but

---

21. Estés, *Women Who Run with the Wolves*, 102.

also suggests that Baba Yaga may not be quite what she seems. She is not simply an old woman living alone in the woods, but a force of nature, a goddess emblematic of the earthy riches of the land itself. Forrester points out Baba Yaga's mystical aspect as an earth goddess: "Baba Yaga appears as an initiatrix, a vestigial goddess, a forest power, and a mistress of birds and animals."[22]

Finally, after Vasilisa completes the tasks Baba Yaga has set out for her, Baba Yaga warns her that to know too much too soon will make one grow old before their time, and asks her if there is anything else she would like to know. This is a test and the crux of the story, where Vasilisa is in the most danger of falling prey to the "consequences" Baba Yaga has hinted at. In this moment, not only has Vasilisa gained enough wisdom to trust her intuition, but she is starting to become discerning. She pauses and checks in with herself. She also seems to understand something of Baba Yaga's warning and that it is connected to the cycles of knowing and initiation, which cannot be rushed.

And what are the consequences that the Yaga hints at? In many of the versions of the story, the consequence is that she will eat Vasilisa and add her bones to her fence. Archetypally, Baba Yaga as wise teacher, initiatrix, and goddess who embodies the wild forces of nature and the cycles of time will literally stop her in her tracks if she is not ready to move to the next step. Figuratively, she will eat her up. Similarly, this can also be a key lesson during the Saturn return. If we get too ahead of ourselves or neglect to pause or to respect the lessons of those who have gone before us, there will be consequences. The Saturn return can be the most humbling and yet paradoxically one of the most important times in one's becoming. It is an initiation in the truest sense of the word. A time when we have entered the dark wood and find ourselves in the hut of Baba Yaga.

Vasilisa has done the work and passed the test and has thus earned the precious fire. Baba Yaga thrusts a skull into her hands and pushes her back over the threshold and sends her on her way, back through

---

22. Forrester, *Baba Yaga*, xxxix.

the forest. While Vasilisa came through the dark wood one step at time, full of fear and trepidation, she now runs through the forest back to her house. She now carries the power and confidence of one initiated. The skull is representative of the wisdom of the ancestors, and now Vasilisa holds that power as she moves forward into the next phase of her life.[23] When she arrives at her old home, the stepfamily is relieved to see her carrying the fire. Any fire they have tried to bring into the house has gone out the moment they brought it over the threshold. But when Vasilisa steps over the threshold holding the skull with the glowing eyes, it stays lit, and they rejoice. Crossing the threshold is a motif rich with archetypal significance and marks a moment of transitioning from one state of being to another. Vasilisa crossed a threshold when she entered the realm of Baba Yaga. After she completed her tasks, she left that otherworldly domain with the fire of knowledge in hand to carry it to the topside world. And now, she crosses yet another threshold as she brings the fire into her home and completes her quest.

The all-seeing eyes of the skull burn the wicked stepfamily to ashes, signifying the end of Vasilisa's old life. Here we see the power of fire in action: it brings light, warmth, illumination, and knowledge, but it also destroys and transforms the old and the outworn so something new can be born. The next morning (morning is wiser than evening) Vasilisa takes the skull and buries it at the foot of an elder tree. Elder is a tree sacred to Frau Holle, another foundational Crone goddess who has some parallels to Baba Yaga. It is said that the dead live beneath the elder tree and that it has healing and regenerative powers.[24] Vasilisa does not just toss the skull away or leave it sitting on the table in the house. She reverently takes this vessel of ancestral knowledge and buries it safely in a place of power. She then locks the house with a key and takes her first steps toward her new life.

---

23. Estés, *Women Who Run with the Wolves*, 106–7.
24. Marija Gimbutas, *The Language of the Goddess* (New York: HarperCollins, 1989), 319.

The symbolism of the key is also of importance. Keys can signify closure or open doors to new experience. Keys are a symbol of power, access, and initiation and feature throughout art and literature as a significant archetype. In the story "Bluebeard," the protagonist is given the keys to every room in the house but is forbidden to use the one that opens the door that would bring her the knowledge that could save her life. In medieval France, the lady of the castle was called the *chatelaine* and, representative of her status, wore a clasp at the waist that held the keys to every room, cupboard, pantry, and strongbox in the house. She literally held the keys to the castle and the control and agency that that implies. Another illustration of the symbolism of keys is the Greek crossroads goddess Hecate, known as the Keeper of the Keys. She is a Light Bearer, unlocking the secret portals of wisdom and carrying a pair of blazing torches that can illuminate the path ahead. So when Vasilisa leaves the house and locks it up with a key, it suggests that she has stepped into a new role: she is now the "woman of the house." She has the authority and power to open and close the doors as she sees fit.

And this is often how it is with the Saturn return. It marks the crossing of a significant threshold, and once one has made their way through the dark wood, stood before their own personal Saturnian teachers, and willingly engaged with the work at hand, they are given the keys. People return from this climactic juncture with more confidence, wisdom, and sure-footedness than they had in their previous life. The Saturn return marks the beginning of a whole new chapter.

Chapter 3

The Saturn Return
Cultivating Authenticity
Age 27 to 30

In ancient times, Saturn was the farthest planet that could be seen with the naked eye, and as such, it marked the edge of the known universe. Because it was the only planet surrounded by rings, Saturn was associated with the concepts of structure, limitation, and boundaries. Astrologically, because of its associations with endings, structure, time, and the natural order of things, Saturn has been related to old age, the skeleton, bones, teeth, and skin. It represents the laws of physical reality and the lessons of living as an incarnate soul in a body on a material plane. Saturn reminds us that time is a nonrenewable resource and that we must spend it wisely. It takes Saturn approximately 29.5 years to revolve around the sun, and it stays in a sign for approximately 2.5 years. Saturn is related to Capricorn and the tenth house.

The Romans saw Saturn as the counterpart of the Greek god Kronos, the son of Ouranos the sky god and Gaia the earth mother, and in mythology there are numerous correspondences between the two. Kronos became the king of the Titans after overthrowing his father Ouranos. Myth tells us that on his mother's urging, Kronos castrated his father with a sickle and threw his testicles into the sea, which caused the separation of earth from sky. From the foam emitted by his severed testicles emerged Aphrodite, goddess of sexual love and beauty. However, family history was destined to repeat itself, and

Kronos learned that he too was to be overthrown by one of his sons, just as he had overthrown his own father. To prevent the prophecy from coming true, he swallowed each of his five children at birth, which included the gods Demeter, Hestia, Hera, Hades, and Poseidon. When his consort Rhea was about to give birth to her sixth child, she conspired with Gaia to devise a plan to save it. After giving birth on Crete, she returned to Kronos, handing him a stone swaddled in rags, which he promptly swallowed. The hidden child was Zeus, who grew up to depose his father and become king of all gods, just as the prophecy foretold.

While many Greek and Roman myths are layered and intertwined, the Roman agricultural god Saturn rules over order, time, seasons, cycles, and the harvest. He taught the people farming and viticulture and was often depicted with a scythe. He presided over a golden age, and was associated with morality, wealth, and plenty.

Saturn is associated with sacred responsibility and rewards for hard work. Archetypally, Saturn is the principle of reality that embodies natural consequences and represents the universal law of cause and effect. Saturn represents *what is*, without illusion. Saturn has many facets and has been called the Lord of the Harvest, Father Time, the Cosmic Taskmaster, the Grim Reaper, and the *Senex*, or wise elder. A difficult transit from Saturn is often a significant reality check that can be a sobering time in our life. Respected astrologer Liz Greene writes, "Saturn symbolizes a psychic process as well as a quality or kind of experience. He is not merely a representative of pain, restriction, and discipline; he is also a symbol of the psychic process…by which an individual may utilize the experiences of pain, restriction and discipline as a means of greater consciousness and fulfillment."[25] Saturn represents the principle behind the way we consciously or unconsciously structure our life and our willingness to work with what we have.

---

25. Liz Greene, *Saturn: A New Look at an Old Devil* (York Beach, ME: Weiser, 1976), 10.

In medieval astrology, Saturn was known as the *Greater Malefic*, the bringer of death and endings. It was related to cold and dry qualities and melancholic humor. Saturn also came to be associated with the devil, or "the man in black" in the Middle Ages. Saturn's archetype was firmly rooted in the material, the dense plane of earthly reality, which was believed to be separate from God, spirit, or the heavenly realm. The earthly realm, including the body, was believed to be susceptible to all manner of "sin," including lust, wantonness, and carnal desires. The saying "money is the root of all evil" is also connected to the idea of the material realm being a source of sin that is somehow detached from spirit. It's also interesting to note that Saturn is directly associated with money and worldly material success. Ironically, this split between the inherent sacredness of earth/nature and the realm of spirit has resulted in the desecration of the earth, our home and mother, which could be termed real evil.

It's not surprising that witches were said to associate with the devil in medieval times. Witches were usually closer to the land, and were said to celebrate rather than reject the pleasures of being embodied. In her book *Traditional Witchcraft: A Cornish Book of Ways* author Gemma Gary explains, "The Devil of the traditional witch is not quite the same thing, of course, as the Satan of 'Churchianity,' but is instead intended as the old chthonic folk-god of the land mysteries and of seasonal changes (particularly the Autumn and Winter months), weather (particularly storms), death mysteries and the unseen forces and gnosis of witchcraft."[26]

In alchemical and Hermetic traditions, Saturn is lead, and the goal of the alchemists was to turn lead into gold. Lead is the base material, the *prima materia*, while gold aligns with the sun. The true goal of the alchemist was not turning actual lead into gold but the transformation of the alchemist at a soul level. Individuation can be understood

---

26. Gemma Gary, *Traditional Witchcraft: A Cornish Book of Ways*, 10th anniv. ed. (London: Troy Books, 2019), 77.

as psychic and psychological wholeness, self-realization, standing in one's power, cocreating with the universe, and consciousness.

In alchemy, the first step toward transformation, *nigredo*, has been compared in analytical psychology to the dark night of the soul, when one comes face-to-face with one's shadow.[27] A significant Saturn transit often feels like a dark night of the soul and brings with it the opportunity to delve deeply into shadow material within our unconscious, as we do the work of turning lead into gold in our own lives. The astrological Sun symbolizes the Self, growth, illumination, and individuation, and after a challenging Saturn transit, we often come to a place of increased self-actualization and authenticity.

As Lord of the Harvest, Saturn is also identified with the adage "you reap what you sow." If you have nurtured your crops, you are likely to receive a better harvest than if you neglect to care for them. Saturn teaches us how we can manifest achievement and results in the outer world through hard work, accountability, and perseverance. Saturn's wisdom shows us that for anything worthwhile, we must put in our time and take measured, practical steps toward realistic goals. When we work willingly with Saturn's medicine, he is an ally who helps us crystallize our life purpose and clarify our sacred responsibility—to ourselves, others, and the collective. If we learn to propitiate Saturn—that is, to give him his just due and work with his lessons—we earn experience, wisdom, and knowledge of life's cycles. Liz Greene writes that Saturn is "the Dweller at the Threshold, the keeper of the keys to the gate, and…it is through him alone that we may achieve eventual freedom through self-understanding."[28]

The First Saturn Return: Age 27–30

Every 29.5 years, Saturn returns to the same position it was when we were born, marking both the end of a cycle and the beginning of a

---

27. Robert Hopcke, *A Guided Tour of the Collected Works of C.G. Jung* (Boulder, CO: Shambhala Publications, 1999), 163.

28. Greene, *Saturn*, 11.

new threshold of maturity. The first Saturn return occurs between 27 and 30, the second between 58 and 60, and, if you're lucky to live that long, the third happens between 88 and 90. The Saturn return is one of the most important junctures in the human life span and the first significant crossroads on the way to becoming an actualized adult. It is a coming-of-age initiation. Saturn spends approximately two and a half years in each sign, and the themes of the Saturn return can often be felt from the time Saturn enters the sign it was in when you were born until the time it leaves. Many begin to feel this shift on the horizon as early as 27, and its effects can last until at least 31. Even longer, if one takes into consideration the integration period that follows a major crossroads transit—many feel the reverberations well into their early 30s as the lessons and insights that arise during the Saturn return are embodied. During this time at the crossroads, it is common to feel lonely, isolated, withdrawn, disconnected, or more serious than usual. Depending on the specifics of our lives, situations may arise that bring feelings of rejection, melancholy, or depression. We are more introspective during the Saturn return, and may feel alone and adrift, cut off from our usual support systems. Many feel exhausted, run down, depleted, and worn out. It's not unusual to feel overwhelmed, discouraged, and self-doubt.

Old goals may begin to feel pointless or no longer as meaningful as they once were. Even long-standing friendships can be questioned, and we can feel abandoned by people we thought would be in our lives forever. On the other hand, we might be tired of the drama or being emotionally drained by playing counselor to friends who are constantly in crisis. As we come to new realizations about what we want and don't want in our lives, we might cut ties with friends whom we've bonded to through substance misuse. Or if you're stuck in the same mindset as you were when you were 21, others might start avoiding you. If this is the case, the Saturn return can be an opportunity to reassess your priorities and get yourself on track. The natural consequences related to how you've been living your life throughout your 20s can be a sobering wake-up call. Sometimes literally. If life has been one long party through your 20s, the Saturn return is often the time to pay the piper. You could lose a job because you've called in "sick" too many times when you've had a hangover. On a more serious note, numerous studies show a peak in overdoses in the late 20s. The infamous "27 Club" underlines this. The 27 Club is a list of actors, musicians, and artists who all died at the age of 27. Included in this depressing club are such well-known celebrities as Robert Johnson, Jimi Hendrix, Janis Joplin, Jim Morrison, Brian Jones, Kurt Cobain, and Amy Winehouse. In 1938, legendary blues singer and guitarist Robert Johnson released the ironically titled "Cross Road Blues" a year before his death at the age of 27. I believe there is a connection with the so-called 27 Club and the oncoming Saturn return, if only that Saturn is connected to natural consequences, as well as the limits of the body.

At the Saturn return you have definitely reached a crossroads in your life. And whether you realize it or not, you are in the midst of an initiation. It's understandable if you are feeling confused, anxious, or melancholy as you enter this liminal space between the worlds. The Saturn return is often connected to making a choice or a difficult decision about the next chapter of your life, and it often entails leaving something behind so you can move forward. This often challenging moment of choice is summed up by author Sylvia Plath in *The Bell Jar:* "I saw my life branching out before me like the green fig tree in the story. From the tip of every branch, like a fat purple fig, a wonderful future beckoned and winked....I saw myself...starving to death, just because I couldn't make up my mind which of the figs I would choose. I wanted each and every one of them, but choosing one meant losing all the rest, and, as I sat there, unable to decide, the figs began to wrinkle and go black, and, one by one, they plopped to the ground at my feet."[29] During the Saturn return, there is often a feeling that even if we make the right choice, there will likely still be mourning for the roads not traveled. But choose we must. And in

29. Sylvia Plath, *The Bell Jar* (London: Faber and Faber, 1977), 80.

becoming a choice maker, we step into our power, set our intention, and feel the relief that comes with making a decision. The very act of choosing has energy and sets the course of the next stage of our life in motion.

The Saturn return is a significant rite of passage that is a game changer for almost everyone. Whereas the early 20s may have been a time to socialize with anyone and everyone, many become more discerning during their Saturn return, choosing more mindfully who they share time with. Some may require times of intentional solitude, preferring to withdraw, reflect, and contemplate. There is a certain feeling of vulnerability that can arise now, a tendency to want to remain hidden, at least while you process the deep changes taking place within. The Saturn return often coincides with a moment of clarity that brings with it an acute realization about the reality of *time*. The sudden realization that your 20s are about to come to an end may dawn on you, and if you've been coasting or in denial or putting things off for a vague "someday," this can be when the proverbial shit hits the fan. This threshold often brings a keen awareness of time that didn't exist until now. You might have the sense that time is running out, or you suddenly realize that you're almost 30, which is perhaps one of the reasons that marriages spike for people in their late 20s or early 30s. Incidentally, in 2018, according to statistics from the US Census Bureau, the average age for a first marriage in the US is 27.8 for women, and 29.8 for men.[30]

Conversely, the Saturn return can also be a notorious time for breakups. And while this is not true for everyone, if you've been in a relationship that's keeping you from growing, it could very well come to an end as you near your Saturn return. If you are in a long-term committed partnership or got married when you were younger, expect your relationship to be tested. On the other hand, some couples embrace the hard work, figure out their priorities, and commit in

---

30. Sheri Stritof, "Estimated Median Age of First Marriage by Gender: 1890 to 2018," the Spruce, December 1, 2019, https://www.thespruce.com /estimated-median-age-marriage-2303878.

a new and significant way by moving in together or getting engaged or married during their Saturn return. However, if you've been keeping a relationship together and hoping your partner will change, you may now come to the realization that it's time to move on. It's also possible that your partner could break up with *you*. And while this is obviously painful, please take heart. In retrospect you will come to realize that the end of that relationship was making space for the love of your life. Be good to yourself and get support, but take comfort knowing that although you can't see it now, someone better is on their way. It's very common during the Saturn return for one relationship to end, followed within a year or two by a significant committed relationship. It's also common that a first child is born during the Saturn return, changing the structure of your life and bringing in the Saturnian themes of commitment and responsibility in a tangible way. Be mindful about this, and if you are in a heterosexual relationship and don't plan to have children (or not yet), practice birth control. I have seen a number of clients become pregnant without intending to (at least consciously) during their Saturn return.

Relationships are not the only life area up for review during the Saturn return. Life direction and career are also often on the table. The Saturn return helps you re-evaluate your priorities, so take a good hard look at your life and make some important, if difficult, decisions. It's not uncommon for people to go back to school or retrain in some way during their Saturn return as they begin to embody the deep changes taking place within.

Whatever your personal specifics, the Saturn return often also pares things down. There can be a letting go (whether you feel ready or not) of anything that is not conducive to your continued growth. At first this release process can be emotionally painful, and you might feel a sense of melancholy, sadness, or even depression. You may have been working toward something that you thought you wanted, only to come up against gatekeepers, dead ends, and roadblocks. The powers that be can loom large during your Saturn return. Saturn rules government and institutions, and they can stop you in your tracks with red tape and paper shuffling, effectively barricading you from moving forward. Saturn is here to help you develop persistence, perseverance, and resilience and paradoxically learn the wisdom of letting go. Toko-pa Turner, author of the book *Belonging*, illustrates the process of letting go beautifully: "There is always a sacrifice to be made on the way to belonging. Whether it is breaking with friends, family, security, or convention, something of real value that you've depended on must be relinquished. This is a ruthless phase of elimination—it strips you of everything that is not alive and growing so that you can find your true way of going in the world. The word 'sacrifice' is not really about self-denial, as we've been taught, but comes from the root 'to make sacred.' In order to make an honest encounter with the unknown, something of great value must be given up, lest we cling to an old version of ourselves. And in making that sacrifice, there is a transfer of a power. In naming and releasing it, we own that which used to own us. The energy locked up in our conformity is liberated for our benefit and conscious use."[31]

Although things might feel hopeless at certain points during your Saturn return, sometimes the only thing to do is to remind yourself that this too shall pass. Patience and perseverance can help, as well as being willing to look at your life from a realistic and objective perspective. Remind yourself that the things that are leaving your life are making space for a new sense of self that is emerging from the ashes of the old. The Saturn return is your celestial wake-up call, a crossroads where you are forced to look at reality. It is the moment of reckoning. Instead of staying stuck in unhelpful patterns, the Saturn return can also be an opportunity to build a rich and meaningful next chapter based on what truly matters to you. The developmental purpose of the Saturn return is to grow you up. It is a milestone to maturity. The more you're living in alignment with what is important to you, the less daunting this crossroads will be. However, if you've

---

31. Toko-pa Turner, *Belonging: Remembering Ourselves Home* (Salt Spring Island, BC: Her Own Room Press, 2017), 75.

been pulling the wool over your own eyes or allowing someone else to do so, you will be forced to confront reality, take stock of your life, and begin to create a new cycle rooted in reality rather than wishful thinking. If you've been brought to your knees with your Saturn return, believe it or not, it is one of the greatest opportunities of your life. It may not seem like it now, but Saturn is a wise teacher that knows just what medicine you need.

Chapter 4

Navigating Your Saturn Return

There's a reason you're feeling lost, alone, and a little bit anxious. Time runs differently in the dark wood. Things might feel surreal, like you've stumbled off the path and aren't quite sure of where you're headed. There are strange twists and turns, and nothing is quite what it seems. But this is exactly where you are meant to be. Believe it or not, this is where you become the hero or heroine of your own story. But you can't rush it. If you try to rush it, you will only find yourself even deeper in the dark forest. Remind yourself that this is an important part of your story, and eventually you'll emerge with cleared vision and hard-won wisdom. In the meantime, put one foot in front of the other and choose wisely. Expect teachers and gatekeepers on the path who will challenge you. Pause and listen well. Do the work and be humble. Be patient and observant. You aren't in Kansas anymore.

Practice Radical Self-Compassion

If you feel like pulling the covers up over your head at times during your Saturn return, you're not alone. If you feel disillusioned, emotional, a lack of clarity, deep grief, or overwhelmed, please remember that this is often a time we come face-to-face with our own vulnerability. The Saturn return is a good time to reflect on self-limiting beliefs and the ways we unconsciously sabotage and block ourselves through fear. Make space for radical self-compassion and be courageous enough to be vulnerable. Fear and anxiety are normal human responses to uncertainty. They are not selfish or even controllable responses in some instances, especially if you have experienced trauma earlier in life. Practice good self-care and don't be afraid to reach out if you're feeling overwhelmed. Please don't shame yourself for your feelings. Although sometimes easier said than done, learning to let go and trust the wisdom of Saturn, no matter how it looks now, can be helpful.

Take Time to Reflect

Whether you like it or not, you may be forced to slow down. Expect obstacles. As frustrating as this can be, use this time to take stock of your life and reflect. How have you structured your life up to this point? What's working for you? What is clearly not working? Start a Saturn return journal and get it out of your head and onto the paper. Are you speaking your truth? Are you showing up with authenticity? Are you clear about what you are calling in? You now have a valuable opportunity for self-reflection, to figure out what is truly important to you. You may find insight in retracing your roots and family patterns. Reflecting on the intersection of oppression and privilege in both our personal past and the collective can provide a bigger picture overview.

Accept Responsibility and Make a Commitment

The planet Saturn is associated with commitment and responsibility. If you've been coasting through your 20s, perennially distracted by surface fluff, or waiting on a sign—this is the sign you've been waiting for. It's time to get real and commit to something that matters, whether that be a relationship, spiritual practice, going back to school, your career, or your own personal growth. Take responsibility for yourself and structure your life in a way that makes sense from a pragmatic perspective.

Tend to the Practical Things

Saturn is all about the practical. If you're feeling exhausted, over-whelmed, or plagued with self-doubt, the remedy is to put one foot in front of the other. Make a list of the practical, everyday things that need to get done, and one by one, methodically check them off. Start with the small stuff if you're feeling overwhelmed, but do start. You will be amazed at the feeling of accomplishment you'll get by doing this. It can also go a long way to soothe your anxiety knowing that you finally filed your tax returns, Marie Kondoed your closet, or simply cleaned the cat box.

Create Healthy Boundaries

Saturn rules boundaries, so don't be surprised if boundaries become a main theme in your life during your Saturn return. Boundaries keep us safe psychologically, emotionally, psychically, and physically. They help define us. They teach others that we have a right to be treated with respect and that our needs matter. They help us determine what we are responsible for and what belongs to someone else. Healthy boundaries support us to say no to unreasonable demands on our time and energy and help us practice good self-care.

If your boundaries are shaky in any area of your life, you'll likely receive multiple opportunities to firm them up during your Saturn return. You will be tested. Expect friends, family, partners, cowork-ers, and employers to push the envelope and try to step over your line in the sand.

How do you know when your boundaries have been crossed? Tune in to your intuition and listen to your body. It's important to remember that when our boundaries are crossed, even in seemingly inconse-quential ways, our bodies and instincts perceive it as a threat. There is innate wisdom in the body, and while mental chatter and self-doubt can be distracting, the body doesn't lie. Your heart might beat faster, your breathing might become shallow, or you might feel tingling in your extremities. You may also feel a tightening sensation in your solar plexus or abdomen. The solar plexus, or *manipura*, chakra is the center of our personal power, will, self-esteem, and identity. Unblocking and balancing this important energy center can be beneficial when working on boundaries and self-assertion. In extreme cases, you may even feel physically sick or out of your body when your boundaries are being crossed, especially in situations where sexual consent has not been given. If you feel resentful, anxious, or guilty, chances are someone is stepping over your line.

When you first begin to create better boundaries, you may feel guilty, anxious, or uncomfortable. You might feel a misguided sense of false compassion for the person who is crossing your boundaries or that you're being unkind by saying no. This is totally normal. If people in your life aren't used to you standing up for yourself, expect guilt trips and pushback. Take a deep breath and calmly stand your ground and speak your truth. If the other person is not taking no for an answer, becomes heated, or keeps pushing their agenda, give yourself permission to end the conversation and take yourself somewhere safe. In time, with most relationships, things can and do get better once you begin to assert yourself. However, there are some who have no respect for other people's boundaries, and one of the Saturn return's main lessons is about becoming more discerning: letting go of people, situations, and things that are not in sync with who you are becoming.

Remember that creating healthy boundaries is a learned skill and something that most of us practice in different ways throughout our lives. Don't be too hard on yourself if you slip once in a while as you learn this new skill. Use it as a learning opportunity and move on, knowing you'll have many more opportunities to practice.

Get Clear on Your Core Values

First of all, let's define "values." In *The Self-Confidence Workbook* authors Barbara Markway and Celia Ampel explain, "Values are the principles that give our lives meaning and allow us to persevere through adversity."[32] Make a list of your core values. Be as honest as you can. No self-judgment. Don't write something down because it sounds good or because it's what society, social media, friends, family, or your inner critic says you *should* value. For example, when I ask my clients about their core values, they invariably begin with "being of service." And while this is certainly a worthwhile value that many people hold dear, it's almost become expected, like you're a bad person if it isn't the first thing you think of. Many of us do want to be of service, but if your whole being yearns to be an artist and explore your inner landscape, it's important to own that (not that you can't be an artist and also be of service). Perhaps you determine one of your core values is better self-care and being true to thine own self. Or beginning a spiritual practice. Or giving yourself permission to feel all your feelings. We talk about authenticity and speaking our truth, but how many of us are walking that talk in real time? The whole point of clarifying your values during your Saturn return is to get down to what matters to *you*, without the voices in your head telling you what should matter.

Remember that Saturn has been called the Cosmic Taskmaster. If you are not being true to yourself, expect a steep price. Saturn is all about consequences—good and not so good—so if you are living your life out of sync with your values, it will become clear very quickly. Again, Saturn also rules time. And although you're a long way off from being old, Saturn's clock is always ticking. The Saturn return is a reminder to live as honestly and as intentionally as possible.

---

32. Barbara Markway and Celia Ampel, *The Self-Confidence Workbook* (Emeryville, CA: Althea Press, 2018), 27.

Sometimes defining our core values is easier said than done, especially when we're trying to discern what's ours and what belongs to someone else. Here are some writing reflections to get you started:

- What do you stand for?
- Name three to six people you admire and explain why. They can include someone you know, someone you would like to know, or a character from a book or film.
- If you could do anything you wanted and know you would thrive, what would that look like?
- How do you want to show up in the world? Describe in detail how you would look if you were living in alignment with what matters to you.
- You are reading your own obituary, far in the future. What does it say?

Slow Down

Saturn is a slow-moving planet and favors careful, deliberate persistence over a hasty, "gettin' it done" mindset. This is the time to take it one step at a time. You may be forced to take it slow, as the Saturn return is a notorious time for unforeseen obstacles, setbacks, and complications. Knowing this in advance may help alleviate some of the stress if things don't work exactly according to plan.

Get Support

There is no doubt that the Saturn return can be a difficult and challenging life passage. Please don't hesitate to reach out for help during this time. You are crossing a serious threshold and part of the nature of a Saturn time is that you may feel isolated and alone. But you are not alone. Talk to friends and family who have already passed through this tumultuous time, find a good therapist you resonate with, or check out a Saturn return blog online to share your fears and read about the experience of others going through it right now. You can also consult with a professional astrologer for a deep dive into your personal Saturn return and how it fits into your overall life purpose. The Saturn return can be marked by depression, and occasionally real trauma can unfold during this time. If this is the case, please seek out a trained and accredited therapist or other mental health professional for perspective.

Don't Be Afraid to Reinvent Yourself

If you've spent the last few years in a career or an education path that seems to have lost its relevance, you are not alone. You have likely changed in some important ways and become more self-aware in the past decade or so. It's the rare individual who knows exactly what they want in life when they are 18 to 20.

The first thing to do if you are daydreaming about another career during your Saturn return is to do some serious self-reflection and a thorough inventory of your core values (see above). Remember how Saturn frowns on anything that is not well thought-out, so do your research and do not rush. Make sure you have all the facts before quitting your day job and that you are not just caught in a fantasy of how great you think life as a traveling festival performer/writer/tarot reader would be. I am the last person to question someone else's dreams, considering what I do for a living, but I have learned some valuable lessons along the way in marrying dreams with reality. The good news is working with Saturn will help you manifest some of your dreams. That means being as realistic as possible, having a plan, and making a serious commitment to what you want to create. Anything less will result in the infamous Saturnian reality check, complete with consequences, disillusion, and disappointment. Also, even in a best-case scenario during the Saturn return, expect obstacles and hard work, and learn to spot the fine line between perseverance and realizing when something is not grounded in reality.

Many people go back to school or retrain in some way around their Saturn return. And while some change their entire life plan, some stay in the same career and level up their education to a master's or doctorate. Others who decided to skip college and travel instead throughout their 20s may enroll in university for the first time. Still others choose to pursue alternative education paths and begin a study of herbalism, death doula work, or astrology. Some decide they want to be self-employed. The important thing is to define what is important to you, do your research, and make sure it's a viable plan. You can then move toward your aspirations with measured steps and full commitment.

If you are considering reinventing yourself, don't discount your transferable skills, education, and life experience to this point. Take stock of all your resources and make a list of everything you know and have to offer. Write it down. It's probably more than you think, and with a little creativity, you can repurpose what you've got and use it in a new way.

It's not uncommon to feel "old" during your Saturn return. And although you're far from old, you are definitely entering a new life phase. If you are considering a different life direction, don't stop yourself because you think you're "too old" to go back to school or start something new. The time is going to pass anyway, so you might as well get something meaningful under your belt when you step across this threshold.

Commit to a Spiritual Practice

Committing to a spiritual practice can help you make sense of the challenges that come up during your Saturn return and can bring comfort, perspective, and a deeper sense of purpose. Whether you practice witchcraft, sacred astrology, yoga, archetypal psychology, breathwork, or meditation or just go for regular mindful walks in nature, spirituality is deeply personal and means something different for everyone. During the Saturn return, it's common to feel a need for guidance and meaning, so it's a perfect time to begin or deepen a practice.

Practice Good Self-Care

In your earlier 20s you may have been able to burn the candle at both ends and shrug it off with a limitless supply of energy. Overworking, overplaying, and still able to get up the next day and do it all again. However, during your Saturn return, you may feel more tired than usual, even exhausted. You might be surprised at the shift in your energy, so it's more important than ever to practice good self-care throughout this time, so you don't become run down. You will need all your resources through this crossroads. One of the best things you can do for yourself now is to set limits. Streamline your diet, take care of your skin, and remember to call your doctor for your yearly checkup. If you don't already exercise, find an activity you like and begin now. Saturn rules the limits of the physical body, and you may start seeing signs that you need to take better care of yourself. This is the perfect opportunity to prioritize a self-care routine that will take you into your 30s looking and feeling your best.

Journal Reflections for Your Saturn Return

As you reflect on your own narrative at this threshold, contemplate the following:

- What insights are you calling in because of what you're going through now?
- Are you investing time in people who you know deep down are not in alignment with who you want to become?
- Are you aware of the ways in which you give your power away? What can you do differently to reclaim it?
- What are the stories that have shaped your worldview? What characters have you particularly resonated with? What qualities do these characters have that are already within you that you can cultivate?
- What fears are holding you back from going after what you want?

- What self-limiting beliefs are you ready to change? Where do they come from?
- What do you feel is stopping you or blocking you? Describe.
- What patterns, behaviors, or mindsets do you know intuitively it is time to let go of?
- If you could have, do, or be anything you want, how would the next chapter of your story look?
- What is important to you now?
- What are you willing to commit to?

Chapter 5

A Magickal Tool Kit for Your Saturn Return

Saturn is a powerful magickal ally to connect with during your Saturn return. Call on Saturn to assist in practical matters, such as finding the perfect home or job, as well as consciously structuring your life in a way that makes sense. Saturn is the planet of manifestation in the material world, so work spells with Saturn to create something important. Aligning with Saturn can also help you change a habit, increase self-discipline, and create a sense of order in your life. Working with the ringed planet can help you identify your purpose, make important decisions, create healthy boundaries, and gain clarity. Work magick with Saturn to find your perfect career, make a commitment, and let go of distractions. Saturn magick can help you find your place in the world and focus on your unique contribution. Spells and rituals for letting go, overcoming fears, and identifying blocks are all enhanced by Saturn. Binding and warding spellwork, as well as psychic and physical protection, are also strengthened. See the Saturn correspondences at the end of this chapter for more ways to work with Saturn as a magickal ally.

Pathworking: Through the Dark Wood

In these uncertain times, it can be difficult to navigate our way through the uncertainty, grief, and rage that infuse the collective at this time in history. It's challenging enough to make our way through the liminal thresholds in our personal lives, but when the collective is also at a crossroads, it takes all of our courage, creativity, and heart to find our way through. Many of us long for a guide to help us through these times of transition.

If you find yourself at a crossroads, trying to make a difficult decision, unsure of your next steps, or currently in the dark forest, it may be time to connect with the Old Woman in the Woods—Baba Yaga—for guidance. The following pathworking is best done at night on the waning moon, or when the moon is in Scorpio or Capricorn. Find a quiet place where you will be undisturbed for about fifteen minutes and turn off your phone. Ground and center in your preferred way and clear the space by burning essential oils or incense (check the correspondences at the end of this chapter for suggestions). Wear unrestrictive clothing and get into a comfortable position. Use pillows for support if needed and a blanket to keep warm and comfortable. Have a journal and a pen ready to record what comes up for you after the journey.

You find yourself on the edge of a deep forest. The sun is setting, illuminating the gleaming white bark of birches, their buds swelling as the land awakens. You step forward and enter the wood. You hear the sound of rushing water, and pockets of white-spotted scarlet mushrooms glow in the deepening shadows.

The sun sets, and you catch glimpses of a crescent moon rising through the trees. Presently, the path intersects, and you find yourself at a crossroads. The path you've been walking has had many twists and turns, and you aren't sure that you could even find your way back to from where you came. Suddenly, you hear the sound of hoofbeats, and like a shadow, someone on a black horse slips past you through the trees. Darkness has fallen now, and the moon rises higher. A raven glides overhead on silent wings and settles in a tree above you.

You come upon a strange little house illuminated in the pale moonlight. You shiver and sense something powerful here, a deep power that is old beyond reckoning. You instinctively know that you have wandered past the bounds of wak-

ing consciousness and have stepped beyond the margins. You feel a keen sense of alertness and uncertainty. Around the hut grows a profusion of tangled nightshades, winding their way between a fence of old bleached bones that glow dully in the pale light of the moon. You know that these are the bones of the ancestors, reverently encircling this place of power, guarding the mysteries that lie within.

An old woman's voice comes from inside the hut, strong and clear: "Why have you come?"

You reflect for a moment, and answer respectfully, "I seek insight, Grandmother."

The door to the cottage creaks open, and an elderly woman steps out onto the porch. But while she appears unfathomably old, her eyes are bright and there is something fierce in her countenance. She narrows her eyes and takes your measure. "Yes, I suppose it is time." She waves for you to enter the gate. You steady yourself and cross the threshold. You walk up the steps and enter the strange little hut. She is tending a kettle on the fire and motions for you to sit at her wooden table. On the counter you see a mortar and pestle and a basket of white-spotted crimson mushrooms. She pours a cup of tea from the kettle and hands it to you. "Drink."

You take the cup in both hands, and inhale the fragrant steam, redolent of earth and decaying leaves.

As you drink the tea, your eyes close, and images begin to arise. The images rise and fall, and you lose all track of time as one vision transforms into the next. Silently, you ask, "What do I need to know for the next steps on my path?" Although you have not spoken aloud, the old woman drops her palms on the table and chuckles softly, "You already have your answer."

She speaks: "This is the insight you have been seeking. You are the hero of this tale. Everything you have ever seen and ever will see is part of your story. This is but a chapter in the book that is your life. This chapter will end in time, and then another will begin. You will cross this threshold, and then another. And then another. One foot in front of the other. The cycles cannot be rushed. Take time to step back and see how it is all connected. For that is how you become wise."

The old woman places something in your hand and closes your fingers around it. She whispers, "Morning is wiser than evening."

You hear hoofbeats and open your eyes just in time to see the flash of some-one riding past the window on a white horse. The first light of dawn seeps into the cottage. The old woman is gone, and the tea has grown cold. You rise from the table and walk out the door, back through the gate, and out into the forest, where the sun is just beginning to rise. You open your hand and see that the old woman has given you an old key. You drop it into your pocket and know instinctively that this is a talisman that will guide you on your next steps. It is up to you to discern which doors it will open.

Ritual: Crossing the Threshold

In his book *To Bless this Space Between Us* the beloved Irish poet, author, priest, and visionary John O'Donohue wrote, "At any time you can ask yourself: At which threshold am I now standing? At this time in my life, what am I leaving? Where am I about to enter? What is preventing me from crossing my next threshold? What gift would enable me to do it? A threshold is not a simple boundary; it is a frontier that divides two different territories, rhythms, and atmospheres."[33] These words beautifully illustrate some key questions that arise during the Saturn return, as we are indeed crossing a significant threshold and marking this rite of passage with contemplation, and ritual can help you witness this cusp in a meaningful way.

Perform the following ritual when the Moon is in one of the *threshold signs* (the mutable signs Gemini, Virgo, Sagittarius, and Pisces). These signs bridge one season into the next. They are shapeshifters connected to transition times and lend their energy to any ritual, ceremony, or magickal working that taps into becoming, transformation, and moving between worlds. Find the time of the next New Moon and try to plan your ritual so it begins just before the new and concludes as the Moon becomes new. If the New Moon occurs in the middle of the night, and waking up to do ritual is difficult, it's still okay to do it the next day. Another good time to do this ritual is at a

---

33. John O'Donohue, *To Bless This Space Between Us* (New York: Doubleday, 2008), 48.

liminal time of day, such as dawn or twilight. The word *liminal* is rooted in the Latin *limen,* which means "threshold." It is an in-between space, neither here nor there, a magical realm of possibility and becoming.

You Will Need

- An old key (Old keys are easily obtained in antique shops, in secondhand stores, or online.)
- An old piece of clothing, shoes, wrap, scarf, etc. that symbolizes a phase of life you are leaving behind
- Small altar (if you are working outdoors, work with what is there: e.g., a flat-topped rock)
- A doorway to symbolize the threshold you are crossing (Alternatively, you can do this ritual outdoors and use a narrow stream that you can safely jump over, a fallen tree across a path, or other natural feature that acts as a threshold. Small pedestrian bridges are also greatly symbolic for crossing a threshold and are often found in parks.)
- Black candle
- Small cauldron, stone mortar, or other fireproof dish
- A new piece of clothing, shoes, wrap, scarf, etc. that symbolizes your new path or identity
- Herbs, incense, or essential oil associated with Saturn to clear your space
- Sharp-tipped small knife, metal skewer, or carving knife to carve the candle
- Paper and pen
- Paper bag

Before the ritual, cleanse your key by burying it in a dish of earth (earth being symbolic of Saturn), preferably overnight on a waning moon. When it is cleansed, charge it with your intent. Hold the key in your hands and visualize it opening doors to new experiences, connections, and knowledge that will guide you on the next steps of your path.

Imbue the key with the intention that it will unlock the right doors, giving you safe passage through the gates of new experience.

When you are ready to do the ritual, put on the item of clothing or shoes that represent a phase of life you are leaving behind. Place the new shoes or clothing on the other side of the threshold. If you are preparing an altar, do this now. Set it up as close to the threshold as possible, in that liminal space between. Refer to the Saturn correspondences at the end of the chapter for altar ideas. Place the key, candle, cauldron, and new item of clothing on the altar. Clear your chosen space and ground yourself. Carve the glyph for Saturn into the candle to represent this milestone, and call in his energy for commitment, perseverance, wisdom, and purpose.

Light the candle (if you are outside, make sure it is safe to do so).

Take some time to contemplate what you are leaving behind. Make sure to acknowledge and thank the things of the past that have led you to this moment and write out what you are leaving on the paper. When you are ready, put the paper into your cauldron or fireproof dish and light it with the candle. Watch as the things of the past are consumed and transformed to ash. This may bring up emotions, and you might shed tears as you say goodbye to the past. Allow yourself time to process your feelings.

When you are ready, pause at the threshold and visualize yourself leaving behind what it is time to release so you can move forward.

Slowly and reverently remove your old item(s) of clothing and thank them for serving you. Place them in a paper bag.

When you are ready, take a deep breath and step across the threshold.

Take a moment to feel the momentous shift that this action symbolizes as you step into your next chapter.

Put on the new item of clothing, and then pick up the key and say,

With this key I open doors
To carry me safe to distant shores
With this key I cross the gate
And in my own hands I hold my fate

Put out the candle, give thanks, and close the ritual.

Place the key on your altar at home or carry it safely with you as a talisman. If it has a loop on the top, you can thread a length of ribbon through it and wear it as a necklace or hang it somewhere to remind you that you hold the key that will open the right doors.

Take the ashes of the past and bury them at a crossroads. Take the paper bag with your old items of clothing and donate them.

Allies and Correspondences for Saturn Times

STONES AND MINERALS: Anthracite (coal), black tourmaline, diamond, epidote, fluorite, fossilized bone, jet, obsidian, smoky quartz, stibnite

FOR GRIEF OR A BROKEN HEART: Emerald, lepidolite, peridot, rhodonite, rose quartz

FOR ENERGY: Bloodstone, carnelian, fire agate, garnet, Herkimer diamond, ruby, sunstone, zircon

ESSENTIAL OILS: Douglas fir, pine, vetiver, cypress, oakmoss

FOR UPLIFTING AND ENERGIZING: Cinnamon, ginger, clove, bergamot, cardamom, basil, juniper, peppermint, dragon's blood, spearmint, benzoin, tangerine, sweet orange, rosemary, frankincense, myrrh

DEITIES: Saturn, Kronos, Baba Yaga, Hecate, Frau Holle, An Cailleach, the Norns, Dagda

COLORS: Black, gray

HERBS: Henbane,* datura,* wolfsbane,* monkshood,* angelica, burdock, comfrey, black hellebore, mullein, shepherd's purse, Solomon's seal, holly, witch hazel, juniper, elderberry (*Indicates baneful plants. These plants are highly toxic, and great care and research should be taken before working with them in any capacity, including handling them.)

PLANT ALLIES FOR SUPPORT: St. John's wort, lemon balm, milky oats, ginseng, *Ginkgo biloba*, schisandra berries, cordyceps, holy basil, maca, eleuthero root, golden root, white oak bark, hops

BACH FLOWER REMEDIES: Wild oat, aspen, beech, cerato, chestnut bud, clematis, elm, gentian, hornbeam, larch, mimulus, mustard, oak, olive, rock rose

SIGNS: Capricorn, Aquarius

HOUSE: 10th

ELEMENT: Earth

TAROT CARD: The Devil

Part 2
The Midlife Transits

Midway upon the journey of our life
I found myself in a forest dark,
For the straightforward pathway had been lost

Dante

Between approximately 36 and 48, you will likely find yourself standing on the edge of the dark forest once again. There are four major life transitions on your horizon, known collectively as the *Midlife Transits,* which occur now and coincide with what society refers to as the "midlife crisis." Each one of these junctures brings up different motifs and serves to further help you on the path to self-actualization. These transits can be profound rites of passage, and if we work with them consciously, they can bring us to a whole new level of soul growth and self-realization. They are transpersonal milestones, psycho-spiritual thresholds, and times of self-discovery, personal growth, and individuation. Psychologist James Hollis writes, "Perhaps Jung's most compelling contribution is the idea of *individuation,* that is, the lifelong project of becoming more nearly the whole person we were meant to be—what the gods intended, not the parents, or the tribe....Our individuation summons each of us to stand in the presence of our own mystery, and become more fully responsible for who we are in the journey we call our life."[34]

Although there will likely be moments of clarity and respite, poignant insights, and deep personal transformation along the way, finding a good therapist, making space for retreat, and getting support are all beneficial during these years of intense individuation. Because these junctures happen so close to one another, and at times even overlap, midlife can sometimes feel like a roller coaster. Deep inner shifts and outer world realities can coincide and change the fabric of our lives. What was so sure for so long can change in a heartbeat, leaving us stranded far from familiar shores. And while these changes can feel sudden, we often find that if we are honest with ourselves, they have likely been brewing beneath the surface for some time.

Midlife can be a notorious time for marriage and long-term commitments. As we wake up to new and emerging aspects of ourselves, we may seek new experiences. Not all marriages end now, obviously,

---

34. James Hollis, *Finding Meaning in the Second Half of Life* (London: Gotham Books, 2005), 10.

but many undergo a time of change to better serve the evolving needs of the relationship. Jobs and careers can change now too, for a variety of reasons. Many have been working much of their adult life in the same career, and inner realizations surfacing into awareness can prompt thoughts of the roads not taken. Old dreams and passions may resurface. Or we may be forced to reevaluate our career because of outer circumstances. Those who have opted to have children may now see those children preparing to leave the nest in the not-too-distant future, triggering a shift in personal identity. Some who have not had children may be hearing the tick of the proverbial clock or feeling grief for what did not come to pass.

Physical changes also begin to occur at midlife. We may notice the first faint lines etching across our face. Metabolic changes that can affect our weight occur. Some women begin to enter perimenopause, signaling a biological shift that can be accompanied by emotional and physiological changes. Declining estrogen can also be linked to insomnia. Some men may be surprised by the first flagging of their virility, as testosterone levels begin to decrease around age 40. Sometimes these physiological changes can trigger anxiety or depression and the pervasive feeling that youth is slipping away, which can lead to a "last chance" feeling. Some obsess about their appearance, while others are drawn into extramarital affairs for illusory affirmation of their desirability. When we stand on the edge of 40, it's not hard to realize that only 20 years ago, we were 20, and in that same amount of time we will be 60. We become keenly aware of how quickly time passes and of all the things we wanted to do that have been left undone. Regardless of gender, we all come to the crossroads now and are called to reflect on what gives our lives meaning, as well as what changes we are willing to make to live in accordance with who we are becoming.

In *The Astrology of Midlife and Aging* Erin Sullivan writes about the liminal nature of midlife: "This place in between is a sacred location wherein we undergo a mysterious self-insemination, gestation, and eventual birth. We are prodded, urged and often forced to grow and change."[35] During the Midlife Transits, we may feel depressed, dissatisfied, anxious, apathetic, restless, or unsure of ourselves as we learn to navigate this next rite of passage.

However, midlife is also an opportunity to truly come into our own, to embrace aspects of ourselves that may have been relegated to the back seat because of family and career obligations. I have had many clients at this juncture sit at my table and express, "I've been taking care of others for so long, I have no idea what inspires me anymore." If this is you, take heart. This is good news. It means you have arrived at the gate of the temple, ready to surrender the ego and allow something new to be born. It is the dark before the dawn, and part of the initiatory process. Just like the first Saturn return at age 29 or 30, taking the attitude of the humble initiate is the only way through the gates. Take a deep breath and prepare yourself, as you are about to awake to inner realizations that will shape the next chapter of your story.

I have used the story of Inanna's descent and return from the underworld to illustrate the common motifs that can arise during the four Midlife Transits. While each of these life passages have their own themes, they occur so closely together (and often overlap) that they are often experienced as a whole. And while the edges of these transits are sometimes blurred and may not correspond exactly in sequential order with the structure of the Inanna myth, they do seem to play out with key elements of the story:

PLUTO SQUARE: Descent—the goddess travels to the underworld.

NEPTUNE SQUARE: Liminal—Inanna is hung on the hook.

URANUS OPPOSITION: Awakening—Inanna is revived.

SATURN OPPOSITION: Discernment—Inanna must make a difficult choice that will serve her continued growth.

---

35. Erin Sullivan, *The Astrology of Midlife and Aging* (New York: Penguin, 2005), 8.

Chapter 6

The Descent of the Goddess

Inanna is a Sumerian goddess whose stories come to us from the ancient land of Mesopotamia. The story of her descent to the underworld is widely considered the world's oldest recorded myth, having been inscribed on clay tablets nearly 5,000 years ago. She was known as the Queen of Heaven and was associated with love, beauty, sexuality, sensuality, fertility, power, and war. The goddess Inanna is also linked to the movements of the planet Venus. Her sojourn to the underworld is reflected by the transits of Venus in the sky, where it sets in the west as the evening star and then rises again in the east as the morning star, completely disappearing and then suddenly reappearing in the heavens. When the planet is invisible, it is said Inanna is in the underworld.

The tale of Inanna's descent has been retold and interpreted countless times, particularly in Jungian and depth psychology circles, as well as in astrological and Pagan communities. And while the myth has often been analyzed through a feminist lens as a model of female empowerment, the story is timeless and archetypal, a powerful symbolic metaphor that resonates with anyone who has ever found themselves in a dark night of the soul, regardless of gender.

And, as we shall see, the descent of Inanna also has many symbolic parallels to the rite of passage we call midlife. Midlife is a time when hidden aspects of the Self emerge, causing us to descend into our own underworld for a time and later resurface, deepened and hopefully wiser than before. Author Diane Wolkstein points out the cathartic potential inherent in a descent: "These rituals give women and men the experience of being reborn on a spiritual plane....Those who do return...become known as shamans and Great Magicians. They carry within them the knowledge of rebirth and often return bringing to their cultures a new world view."[36] The story of Inanna's descent and rebirth is layered with archetypal insight that can be useful during the Midlife Transits, or at any time we find ourselves in a descent.

Inanna, Queen of Heaven, hears something just outside her awareness that captures her attention. Her sister Ereshkigal, Queen of the Underworld, is in mourning. Inanna rises and decides that she will go and visit her sister in her underground realm, something she has never done before. Something no one has ever done, if they wish to come back to the land of sun and sky. She carefully prepares for her journey to the land of the dead, taking care to array herself in a manner befitting her station as the Queen of Heaven and Earth. On her head, she places her crown. She combs her dark hair and adorns herself with the royal lapis beads. She dons layered strands of beads. She steps into the robe of queenship and adorns her eyes with kohl. Next, she fastens on a fitted breastplate that enhances the ripe curves of her body, and she encircles her wrist with a golden bracelet. Last, she takes up her lapis measuring rod and line.

Thus prepared, Inanna sets out on the road to the gates of the underworld with her friend and loyal maidservant, Ninshubur, at her side. Knowing that the underworld is fraught with danger and that no one has ever returned to tell the tale of their time in the Great Below, she instructs Ninshubur to appeal to the gods for help should she not return in three days. Sending Ninshubur away, she continues to the outer gate of the underworld alone. As she arrives, she knocks boldly upon the door and speaks in a commanding voice, "Open the

36. Diane Wolkstein and Samuel Noah Kramer, *Inanna, Queen of Heaven and Earth* (New York: HarperCollins, 1983), 156.

door!"[37] Neti, the guardian of the Great Below, appears and asks why she has come. Inanna answers that she has come to attend the funeral rites of her sister's husband. Neti tells Inanna to stay at the gate and goes to speak to the queen of the underworld to relay the message. Neti descends to the underworld and tells Ereshkigal that her sister, Inanna, Queen of Heaven, waits outside the gates. He describes how Inanna has prepared herself for the journey, arrayed in the garments of her station, including the seven talismans. Ereshkigal is most displeased and tells her chief gatekeeper to bar the seven gates to the underworld. She instructs him to let Inanna through one by one, but as she passes through each gate, she must leave behind one of her royal garments.

Neti returns to the outer gate of the palace and bids Inanna enter. As she enters the first gate, he takes the crown from her head.

"What is this?" asks Inanna.[38]

Neti replies, "Quiet, Inanna, the ways of the underworld are perfect. They may not be questioned."[39]

At each of the six remaining gates to the underworld, Inanna is instructed to relinquish one of the emblems that identifies her status in the topside world.

Inanna enters the throne room, stripped bare and humbled. Ereshkigal is not pleased that Inanna has entered her realm uninvited. She is outraged that Inanna has felt entitled to array herself in the garments of her station and enter the underworld. Ereshkigal strikes her dead and hangs her on a hook to rot in the darkness.

When her mistress doesn't return in three days, Ninshubur beats the drum and tears at her face and clothes in mourning. She approaches the gods for assistance as she was instructed, but one by one they turn her away, exclaiming that Inanna got what she deserved. How could she dare be so entitled as to think she could

---

37. Wolkstein and Kramer, *Inanna, Queen of Heaven and Earth*, 55.

38. Wolkstein and Kramer, *Inanna, Queen of Heaven and Earth*, 57.

39. Wolkstein and Kramer, *Inanna, Queen of Heaven and Earth*, 58.

enter the realm of the dead and return to the land of the living? Finally, Ninshubur comes upon the god Enki, who shows compassion for Inanna. From the tip of his fingernail, he conjures two genderless beings to help bring Inanna back from the land of the dead. To one he gives the food of life and to the other he gives the water of life. He instructs them to go to the underworld and seek out Ereshkigal, who is groaning like a woman in labor; she lies uncovered and her hair is disheveled. Enki tells them that when they find her, they are to show compassion for her pain, and she will offer them a gift. These tiny beings slip unnoticed into the underworld to find Ereshkigal. They sympathize with her pain, and startled by their compassion, she grants them whatever they wish. They reject her offerings of a field filled with grain and a full river and ask instead for the corpse rotting on the hook. Ereshkigal grants them their wish, and the tiny beings sprinkle Inanna with the food and water of life, and she rises.

On her way back to the topside world, Inanna is accompanied by demons of the underworld who must bring back a sacrifice in her place. As they walk through the gate, the first person they encounter is loyal Ninshubur, dressed in mourning rags. She throws herself at Inanna's feet in relief when she sees her beloved mistress. The demons turn to take Ninshubur as a substitute, but Inanna refuses to sacrifice her. Ninshubur is a friend, a confidant, and a warrior who fights at her side. Each person they encounter is dressed in mourning rags and throws themselves at the feet of their goddess when they see her, so she forbids their being taken as a sacrifice. Finally, they come to the big apple tree, where her husband Dumuzi sits on his throne. He is dressed brightly in his kingship garments and does not rise when he sees Inanna. "Take him!" she cries. "Take Dumuzi away!"[40] The demons seize arrogant Dumuzi and drag him away as sacrifice to the queen of the underworld.[41]

---

40. Wolkstein and Kramer, *Inanna, Queen of Heaven and Earth*, 71.

41. Wolkstein and Kramer, *Inanna, Queen of Heaven and Earth*, 53–71.

How is a 5,000-year-old myth symbolic of the time we call midlife? To begin with, at some point around the Pluto square, approximately between 36 and 48, we begin to hear the call of something outside ourselves. Previously hidden aspects begin to emerge from our unconscious, vying for our attention and changing how we respond to our lives. Sometimes something initiates the descent, whether it be a quest for more meaning, an illness, the loss of a job, a relationship, or a sense of identity. Inanna may be the queen of heaven, but the underworld is not her realm. Until she is receptive to the call of the Great Below, she has no knowledge of it.[42] And the same can be said for us when we begin the sojourn that is midlife. We don't know what we don't know until we take the first step into the unknown.

As we stand on the precipice of this rite of passage, we may feel intuitively that we need to prepare for something, although we may not yet be sure what that might be. Like Inanna, we gather the talismans that make us feel powerful, those things that compose our ego self until now: self-image, beauty, desirability, education, worldly success. We don these outer symbols of identity and status as a sort of armor, in hopes that they will protect us, wherever we're going. But in a descent, those things of the topside world fall away or are stripped from us one by one, until we too find ourselves in the underworld. And as each one of our talismans are removed, we may feel bewildered, vulnerable, raw, or indignant. *"What is this?"* But the more we try to hang on to what is no longer viable in our lives, the harder this passage can be.

When Ereshkigal hears that Inanna is waiting outside the gate to enter her realm, she is displeased. Inanna represents heaven and earth, the land where the sun shines, and the fertile crops grow. She is linked to sensuality and conscious power. Ereshkigal, on the other hand, is the queen of the dreary land of the dead. But she wasn't always consigned to the darkness. Ereshkigal once lived in the land

---

42. Wolkstein and Kramer, *Inanna, Queen of Heaven and Earth*, 156.

above and was a goddess of grain.[43] She represents the disowned parts of ourselves that have been relegated to the shadow, the unconscious aspects of self that for whatever reason were not deemed fit to see the light of day, as well as symbolizing "raw instinctuality split off from consciousness."[44] Consequently, we often find rage in the shadow, as well as a sense of abandonment and deep sorrow. At midlife, we have roughly 40 years of repressed shadow material that can emerge now to be witnessed.

When Inanna enters the throne room, she has been stripped of everything that signifies her identity and status as the queen of heaven. She has no power in the underworld, and her talismans cannot help her. Ereshkigal strikes her dead, hanging her on a hook to rot. When we find ourselves in a descent, which often happens during these transits, we too can feel annihilated. None of our usual supports can help us in the underworld. This is the time when we truly feel we are in the dark night of the soul. All we can do is surrender and wait.

But even in the depths, there is a part of us that can act on our behalf. It has often been interpreted that Inanna and Ereshkigal are two sides of the same goddess or psyche. But there is a third aspect in Ninshubur, the loyal companion who fights at Inanna's side. When her mistress does not return in three days' time, Ninshubur sounds the alarm and appeals to the gods for help, thus saving Inanna's life. Author Sylvia Brinton Perera explains Ninshubur's role: "Psychologically, she seems to embody that small part of us that stays above ground while the soul descends, the still conscious and functioning aspect of the psyche which can witness the events below and above and feel concern for the fate of the soul."[45] This is the part of us that

---

43. Thorkild Jacobsen, *The Treasures of Darkness: A History of Mesopotamian Religion* (New Haven, CT: Yale University Press, 1976), 99.

44. Sylvia Brinton Perera, *Descent to the Goddess: A Way of Initiation for Women* (Toronto: Inner City Books, 1981), 23.

45. Perera, *Descent to the Goddess*, 63.

even in our darkest hour takes care of us and makes sure the practical things of our lives are at least somewhat sound. The part that calls our best friend or our therapist and maintains a lifeline to the outside world when we are deep in the throes of shadow work.[46]

After appealing to several gods for help and being turned away, Ninshubur finally comes upon Enki, the God of Wisdom. Enki fashions two beings that are small enough that they can slip into the underworld without being seen. He tells them that Ereshkigal is alone and crying out like a woman in labor; further, she is not honored (she lies uncovered in her vulnerable state). He tells them that when they find her thus, they are to offer her compassion, to witness her in her state of abandonment. And this is the key to how we can best respond when we come face-to-face with our own shadow: by offering compassion and bearing witness to those parts of us that have been abandoned, forsaken, and consigned to the underworld of the unconscious. By meeting our vulnerability and honoring our sacred dark, we reclaim the fragmented self.

In gratitude for their compassion, Ereshkigal grants the tiny beings the corpse on the hook, and they sprinkle her with the food and water of life, thus reviving Inanna. She is reborn. As she makes her way back to the sunlit world, she is followed by demons of the underworld whose job it is to bring back a sacrifice or substitute. Inanna forbids their taking Ninshubur, as she is the one who saved her life. She stays their hand at each person they encounter, for they are clearly mourning the loss of the queen of heaven. But when they come to her husband, Dumuzi, sitting proudly on his throne and not deigning to rise when he sees his wife is alive, she cries out that he is the sacrifice that should be taken to Ereshkigal. Dumuzi represents that which no longer serves us, and when we come up out of a personal descent, we too must recognize and let go of that which is not supportive of our evolving self.

---

46. Perera, *Descent to the Goddess*, 63.

When Inanna surfaces from her ordeal in the underworld, she has been harrowed and is now tempered. She is matured. She has integrated the dispossessed aspects of herself and is deepened. Wolkstein illustrates that "it is the Great Below, and the knowledge of death and rebirth, life and stasis, that will make of Inanna an 'Honored Counselor' and a guide to the land."[47] Similarly, we are also transformed by our time in the underworld: we step across the threshold and return initiated, with more wisdom than we had before.

47. Wolkstein and Kramer, *Inanna, Queen of Heaven and Earth*, 156.

Chapter 7

The Pluto Square
Descent
Age 36 to 48

Pluto was discovered in 1930 and is identified as the Roman counterpart of Hades, the Greek god of the underworld. Although it was reclassified as a dwarf planet in 2006, in astrology it is identified as a cathartic force that cannot be ignored. Pluto represents the shadow side of life, the hidden undercurrents that run beneath the topside world, and is intimately connected with the mysteries of sex, death, and rebirth. Pluto corresponds with hidden trauma and the depths of human experience, as well as the hard-won wisdom that comes with having made a journey through the underworld and back. Pluto speaks to soul growth and spiritual evolution, as well as shadow aspects, such as obsession, manipulation, and primal instincts including repressed rage, grief, and desire. Pluto is connected to the idea of purging or unearthing buried or repressed material so it can be transformed and used as compost for new growth. Wherever Pluto is located in the birth chart often shows a portal where one will go through intense experiences that can lead to profound transformation and bring one into a sense of one's own power. Pluto takes 248 years to move around the sun, and because of the nature of its orbit, it stays in a sign for approximately 12 to 31 years. It is aligned with Scorpio and the eighth house.

In order to grasp the archetypal resonance of Pluto, it's helpful to understand his mythic dimensions as Hades, Lord of the Underworld.

In Greek mythology, Hades was the oldest son of Kronos and Rhea. He and his brothers Zeus and Poseidon overcame the Titans, the old generation of gods, and drew lots to see who would rule which realm. Zeus received the sky, Poseidon the sea, and Hades the underworld. Thus, the Olympic pantheon of gods was born. His name means "the unseen one," as his domain was beneath the earth, and he only came to the daylit surface world twice—once to claim as his bride the unwitting maiden Kore or Persephone, who became queen of the underworld, and once in order to heal a wound. He was also known by the epithet *Pluton,* meaning wealthy, as he ruled the realm from which all manner of riches sprang, including precious metals and the fertile earth from where crops emerged. He was the god associated with buried treasure. As god of the dead, Hades kept the balance, and no living being was exempt from his laws.

When we have a powerful Pluto transit, it often coincides with a death of the ego, as old versions of ourselves are laid waste. We can feel brought to our knees during a major Pluto transit, as Pluto can tear down the old existing forms of our lives, so that we have no choice but to begin the work of creating something new. Pluto is connected to the tarot card Death and, as such, symbolizes important endings and transformation. And even though pulling the Death card usually heralds new beginnings and eventual rebirth, the initial loss that accompanies Death should not be overlooked. It is a sacred time of initiation, and grieving is an important part of the process that needs to be honored before we are admitted through the gateway into new life. Neglecting to give death its proper due, whether it be the death of a phase of life, a relationship, or even a loved one, pushes unprocessed feelings into the shadow. And whatever is pushed to the shadow may rise up in unexpected ways at inappropriate times to be dealt with.

Just like Hades, Lord of the Underworld, Pluto is impartial when it is time for something to die, which can be the most frightening part of a Pluto transit. The destruction and dissolution of existing forms in our lives can feel impassive and cold. Saturn too can be cold and detached, but Saturn is an earthy principle. Because Pluto is the farthest planet from the sun, there is a remoteness about it that can feel distant and unknowable. During a Pluto transit, we can feel disconnected and cut off from everything that made sense a short time ago. There is a reason Pluto is associated with death.

When we have a significant Pluto transit, occasionally death is, in fact, literal and not metaphorical. I don't say this to frighten anyone, and by no means does a Pluto transit usually herald a physical death, but it can. Astrology cannot predict exactly what form a transit will take, but it can give us timing and a clear picture of the themes that will arise. Pluto is not only about death, but the rebirth that can only come after a dark night of the soul. Pluto illuminates the shadow and brings to the surface that which has been repressed, hidden, and out of view. Pluto also regenerates and heals old trauma and wounding, but only after the cleansing fires of purification, so new growth can begin.

Pluto transits are usually times marked with volcanic intensity. Whether it is playing out in your life as a deep internal shift or manifesting in your outer world (or likely both), there is often a primal ferocity connected to Pluto that shows up as extremes. British astrologer and author Clare Martin explains, "As Pluto becomes active an intensity starts to build deep in the unconscious until the tension of the suppressed energy becomes unbearable. Inherited, ancestral, and collective material emerges from the unconscious and threatens to consume us."[48]

Sometimes, we project our Pluto onto others, and we find ourselves the victim of Plutonian intensity coming from outside ourselves. We may meet Pluto in intense, extreme people or situations. It's as if the deeper self is conspiring with the universe to help us step into our power by presenting us with the most challenging circumstances possible. Power struggles that have a peculiar life or death undertone are common during Pluto transits. The deep lesson woven into these

---

48. Clare Martin, *Alchemy: Soul of Astrology* (Swanage, UK: Wessex Astrologer, 2020), 73.

junctures is to learn to own our power in a clear and conscious way. There will likely be no shortage of opportunities for you to do so. At the same time, Pluto will also show you where reluctance to be in your power contributes to passive-aggression and buried resentment and rage, which can lead to toxic relationships. Pluto times are shadow work times. Whatever you have repressed or would prefer not to look at may be impossible to avoid. Pluto transits usually last between a year and a half and two years. They are gateways for profound personal transformation, and during its journey, Pluto will strip you down and polish you until you gleam like a diamond.

The Pluto Square

The Pluto square is the first of the Midlife Transits and occurs when transiting Pluto forms a square aspect to your natal Pluto. Unlike the other transits mentioned in this book, the ages for the Pluto square vary quite widely from generation to generation, because of the nature of Pluto's orbit. Those born with Pluto in Leo, Virgo, Libra, and Scorpio (between 1937 and 1995) will experience their Pluto square during midlife (at some point between the ages of 36 and 44), while those born after 1995 will experience it considerably later. For example, those born with Pluto in Sagittarius (between 1995 and 2008) will have their Pluto square at around age 48, and those born with Pluto in Capricorn (between 2008 and 2023) will have their Pluto square between the ages of 58 and 59.[49] If you'd like to pinpoint the dates of your Pluto square, consult with a professional astrologer, or download a transit app such as Time Passages or Time Nomad. So unless you are reading this book after the year 2043, you will be experiencing this rite of passage as a midlife transit.

Numerous astrologers, including Liz Greene and Howard Sasportas, have compared the Inanna myth to the transit of Pluto through the birthchart, and when we reach this crossroads, it is true that we

---

49. Sullivan, *The Astrology of Midlife and Aging*, 124.

often find ourselves drawn into an underworld of sorts.[50] The myth of the descent of the goddess draws some profound archetypal parallels that especially correspond to the Pluto square. Like Inanna, we may hear the call of something outside our awareness, and decide to heed that call. We may sense unconsciously that it is time to face our shadow, to integrate the treasure that lies in the dark. However, even if we think we're in control of our personal descent, we are not. In fact, relinquishing control of the ego is the whole point, as Inanna discovers at the seven gates when she is stripped of all the symbols of her power in the topside world. Surrender when entering the underworld is the only way to transformation at a soul level.

Like Inanna facing Ereshkigal, the Pluto square brings us face-to-face with our own shadow, as well as our projected shadow that we meet in others. It is a rite of passage that can harrow and temper us, bringing us to a whole new level of wisdom and personal power that could not be obtained any other way. Like all significant transits, we will each experience the archetypes in our own unique ways, according to the lessons we came here to learn and the specifics of our own lives.

However, most feel raw, exposed, and deeply vulnerable during their Pluto square. Most of us experience a death of sorts, whether it be a relationship, a sense of self, a way of life, or occasionally, someone close to us, which can immerse us in the underworld without warning. Intense emotions can shake us to our core, long-buried rage and insecurities can surface, and we may be pulled into deep grief. It's important to remember that grief can arise even if we have not experienced the physical death of someone close to us. The end of a treasured relationship and of outworn personas as well as the realization of things that did not come to pass can all be roads to transformative and cathartic grief. David Kessler is one of the world's

---

50. Liz Greene, *The Astrology of Fate* (Boston, MA: Weiser, 1984), 39; Howard Sasportas, *The Gods of Change* (Swanage, UK: Wessex Astrologer, 2007), 200–4.

foremost experts on dying and grief and cowrote two books with Elisabeth Kübler-Ross, the psychiatrist who originated the concept of the five stages of grief in her seminal work, *On Death and Dying*. In his recent book, *Finding Meaning: The Sixth Stage of Grief,* Kessler writes, "We want to find meaning. Loss can wound and paralyze. It can hang over us for years. But finding meaning in loss empowers us to find a path forward."[51]

If we are feeling grief for any loss during our Pluto square, it is important to honor that grief. To sit with it, let it move through us, and fully feel it, to allow ourselves to be transformed by it. We need to extend compassion and nonjudgment to ourselves and create the space for alchemy. Pluto is also associated with rebirth, and we must remember that rebirth only comes after we have surrendered to the ending of what came before.

All Pluto transits have the tendency to bring things to the surface. And this is especially true when Pluto is making aspect to itself. Think of a challenging Pluto transit like an abscessed tooth. Its function is to alert us that there is something toxic beneath the surface that needs to be expelled and cleansed so it can be healed. Whatever we have repressed or denied and relegated to the shadow can emerge now, especially highly charged emotions connected to old wounds. It's common for a person or a situation outside us to act as a catalyst to reopen these wounds, triggering long-buried feelings that come rushing forth with all the energy of the original trauma. Unintegrated and unacknowledged pain, grief, rage, injustice, abandonment, betrayal, shame, and guilt can explode into awareness now, demanding to be witnessed.

Now is the time for shadow work. Attempting to keep repressed material contained or controlled is a recipe for disaster that can lead to toxic secrets, passive-aggression, and covert acting out. Even if you don't feel safe talking about your shadow with friends and family, you

---

51. David Kessler, *Finding Meaning: The Sixth Stage of Grief* (New York: Scribner, 2019), 2.

still need to process the material that arises. Finding a good therapist can be more important now than ever. Pluto is connected to secrets, often of a sexual nature, and some with unprocessed shadow material are drawn now to clandestine affairs and other secret sexual activities. The adult entertainment and sex industries are rife with clients acting out their repressed secret shadow material. Remember that any archetype or transit can play out as a projection. In other words, it may not be you who is acting out Pluto's shadow but someone in your life. But with Pluto, nothing can be contained or controlled forever: it must surface, and surface it will.

At the same time, the Pluto square can be a time of intense sexual awakening. If we are honest with ourselves and work willingly with the shadow aspects that arise, we might find that we can embrace an authentic sexuality for the first time in our lives on our own terms. This threshold can be an opportunity to heal sexual trauma and reclaim sexual sovereignty. And while this can be one of the most empowering and freeing things you can do, it can also be emotionally challenging and triggering. Please don't hesitate to seek support if you need it.

As intense and frightening as the Pluto square can seem, its purpose is to help you release toxic patterns, face and integrate your shadow, let go of and release trauma, and step into your true power. It might be said that the core purpose of the Pluto square is to find meaning in our suffering so that we find what Jungian psychologist Robert Johnson called "the gold in the shadow."[52] Although Pluto transits can be harrowing, there is a fierce beauty with Pluto that is often overlooked. Once we have undergone its lessons, Pluto brings regeneration, healing, and a sense of new empowerment. It shines a light into dark places so we may see what needs to be released so we can grow. We surface from our time in the underworld with increased depth and wisdom. We begin to let go of false symbols of power and

---

52. Robert A. Johnson, *Owning Your Own Shadow: Understanding the Dark Side of the Psyche* (New York: HarperCollins, 1991), 8.

prestige, stop comparing ourselves so much with others, and lean into a new sense of self. We must remember that one of Pluto's core symbols is the phoenix, the mythical bird connected to rebirth and resurrection who dies each night and is reborn again with the sunrise from her own ashes.

Chapter 8

Navigating Your Pluto Square

Whether you are ready or not, Pluto will invite you to witness your shadow in no uncertain terms. In Jungian psychology the shadow is the unconscious aspect of the psyche. Jung writes, "Everyone carries a shadow and the less it is embodied in the individual's conscious life, the...denser it is."[53] In my opinion, some aspects of the new age movement have done a gross disservice to seekers by focusing wholly on the light at the expense of recognizing and embracing the shadow. A preoccupation with "lightwork" and "high vibes only" is not only pretentious, privileged, and potentially racist, it is unrealistic and can be psychologically harmful. It also misses the point that also contained within the shadow is a wealth of hidden talents, passions, and abilities we may not even be aware of.

As you move into your Pluto square, your task is to begin to integrate aspects of your unconscious into your conscious life so you can move toward wholeness. Until you do the work of accepting and integrating your shadow, you will likely find it projected onto others, and you will encounter people, situations, and events that trigger you. Until we get acquainted with our shadow, it can be an unconscious driving force beneath many of our behaviors, perspectives, and cognitions, which can result in self-sabotage. An unintegrated shadow

---

53. C. G. Jung, *Psychology and Religion*, vol. 11 of *Collected Works of C. G. Jung* (New Haven, CT: Yale University Press, 1938), 131.

can manifest as feelings of "not enough," distorted expectations in relationships, and inappropriate defense mechanisms. It can also be behind anxiety, obsessions, compulsions, addictions, and buried rage. Do you have an irrational fear of rejection or repeatedly find yourself the victim of others who seem more powerful than you? Do you feel that your creativity is blocked and you are not sure why? Acting out, constantly finding yourself in the center of drama, engaging in unwanted behaviors as if on auto pilot, being drawn into unhealthy relationships, and repeating the same old patterns are all symptoms of an unintegrated shadow.

Embracing your shadow will help you reclaim lost aspects of your fragmented self. You will have greater clarity in relationships and your emotions. Accepting your shadow will help you let go of unhelpful patterns and habitual ways of reacting. You will come from a place of more authenticity as you create healthier boundaries and improve communication with the people in your life. You will cultivate a greater sense of self-worth and joy as you begin to access the gold in the shadow. As you dive into shadow work, try not to judge yourself or what comes up. Have compassion for yourself. Remember, a lot of what gets pushed into the shadow happened at an early age, when it was a survival mechanism. You wouldn't get angry at a child for tucking away their feelings. Shadow work can be hard work, but the rewards are great.

Know When to Retreat

When snakes shed their skin, they tend to do so in private, as they are at their most vulnerable. The purpose of shedding, or *ecdysis*, is because they are growing, and their old skin no longer fits. The symbolism of the snake shedding its skin is connected to regeneration and rebirth, and much like the snake, when we undergo a significant Pluto transit, we too are shedding old skins because we are growing. Many feel intensely sensitive during this time and require periods of privacy, particularly if we are undergoing a time of grief. We may feel stripped bare, exposed, and defenseless during the Pluto square. It's important to find a way to take space from our everyday lives and the prying, if well-meaning, eyes of others. Depending on the specifics of your life, this may or may not be easy. For some, getting away for a few days or a week at a time can be helpful. If you are unable to take that much time, even closing the door to your room and letting others know you prefer to be undisturbed when the door is shut can help. Take what space you can, even throughout the day if possible, so you have the time you need to reflect, regenerate, and heal while you are undergoing the demanding process of rebirth.

Honor Your Grief

Grief is sacred territory. And, while of course grief is not limited to significant Pluto times, it is a hallmark that often does arise now, in different ways for everyone. Although the loss of a loved one is undeniably a time when we experience grief, the guises of loss are many. Some experience the loss of a phase of life or of their identity when they lose a job, or they realize they are on the cusp of 40. Others experience loss when a marriage or significant relationship ends. It's important to take time to witness a loss. Do not judge yourself for the depth of your feelings or succumb to internal or external pressure to just hurry up and get over it. Rituals for grief and closure can be immensely therapeutic now. Psychotherapist Francis Weller eloquently describes the sacred nature of grief: "Every one of us must undertake an *apprenticeship with sorrow*. We must learn the art and craft of grief, discover the profound ways it ripens and deepens us…. Facing grief is hard work….It takes outrageous courage to face outrageous loss. This is precisely what we are being called to do."[54]

---

54. Francis Weller, *The Wild Edge of Sorrow* (Berkeley, CA: North Atlantic Books, 2015), xxii.

Sacred Creative Therapy

My Pluto square coincided with the end of a relationship. I felt like I had entered the underworld in a visceral way, taking daily solitary walks on the gray and desolate shores of my home in the Pacific Northwest for hours on end. I accredit my eventual surfacing from the underworld to the only thing that helped me make sense of it all: a deep dive into what I came to call "sacred creative therapy. My first attempts at releasing my sorrow onto paper were of lonely women with eyes closed or tucked in fetal positions, nestled in the roots of trees. There were lots of poppies and skulls and other symbols of death woven into the borders of every painting. I would forget myself for hours, losing track of time and finding solace in my work. In time, my work began to take on a new quality. I still painted women, but now their eyes were open. Some of them had wings or hair of flames. Sacred hearts replaced the skulls. The power of sacred creative therapy is transformative.

My first attempts at releasing my sorrow onto paper were of lonely women with eyes closed or tucked in fetal positions nestled in the roots of trees. There were lots of poppies and skulls and other symbols of death woven into the borders of every painting. I would forget myself for hours, losing track of time and finding some semblance of solace in my work. One of my most engrossing projects at the time was the transformation of an old book—a gift from my ex when we first got together. I covered the book in purple velvet that I cut from the skirt that I wore when we first met. Inside, I glued old train tickets and oak leaves picked up on our walks together. I burned the edges of poems we had written each other when we lived on opposite sides of the world and glued those in too. Interspersed with all of these were pre-Raphaelite images torn from art magazines, that seemed to tell the tale of our ill-fated love. It became a thing of beauty that enabled me to heal and move on.

In time, my work began to take on a new quality. I still painted women, but now their eyes were open. Some of them had wings or hair of flames. Sacred hearts replaced the skulls. The power of sacred creative therapy is transformative. Only you ever need see what you create. If you are now in a descent, I encourage you to go to an art supply store and give yourself the gift of creative materials. It doesn't matter if you don't consider yourself an artist or have never done this before. Spread your materials out on a table and take some time for yourself. You can treat this time as a ritual, and clear your space first, clarify your intent, and light a candle. Put on some music, or work in intentional silence, and begin. There are no rules, and no judgment. You can set a timer if you wish or work until you feel complete. If you allow yourself to become immersed and make it a regular practice, sacred creative therapy will work its medicine.

Release and Let Go

One of the functions of Pluto is to draw out poison. Although this process can be painful, it is a necessary action that brings to the surface whatever needs to be released. You can work with this natural purpose of Pluto by physically cleansing your home, workspace, and body, similar to homeopathic medicine. Sorting your things and decluttering can be powerful practical magic that works on an energetic level. You can start by making two piles: one to keep and one to donate or give away. You may be surprised at the depth of feeling that arises as you pick up each item and make your decision. You might also come up with a dozen excuses for why you cannot possibly part with certain items, and it might take a few attempts before you are able to go through all your things. Do not feel pressured to give away items that are truly precious to you or that hold layers of meaning. There is also no rush to this process. But do begin. It will give you a powerful feeling of lightness and energy that you may have not felt in a long time. Perhaps because I am a so-called Plutonian (lots of Scorpio and significant Pluto aspects), I've always had a knack for purging what I no longer need or want. I taught my son this valuable skill when he was three years old, and to this day he makes his two piles on a semiannual basis, which he has ceremoniously dubbed "like it or slag it." I've had friends and family ask me to help them purge their closets, garages, and attics, and they beg me to "be gentle." However, my rule has always been you don't have to give it all away. It can be very meditative and affirming as you sort through your piles and silently witness, honor, and thank each item for its role in your life. Remember that you are attached to the physical things in your life by energetic lines of connection. Sometimes it is no longer appropriate to keep those connections, as in the case of a painful breakup. Again, go gentle. There are other instances, though, when you will find you want to keep those golden threads of connection—perhaps you have a vase or a piece of embroidery gifted to you by your grandmother—and there is no reason you should feel obligated to give away those things imbued with meaning.

Physical cleaning of your space can also be very therapeutic during Pluto times. Get out your broom and sweep the floors, dust every corner, and tackle those chores you've been putting off. After you have cleaned, you can energetically cleanse your space by burning purifying herbs such as hyssop, juniper, and rosemary. Finally, cleansing your body can also help facilitate Pluto's action. In fact, you can really think about the Pluto square as one big physical and spiritual detox. There are many gentle healthy cleanses to choose from that range from simply eliminating sugar, alcohol, and processed foods from your diet to herbal cleanses formulated especially for this purpose. Some helpful herb and plant allies for cleansing include burdock, milk thistle, dandelion, and turmeric. If you are in doubt, consult an herbalist or a naturopath. You can also purify, detox, and cleanse your auric body by bathing with or burning essential oils such as rosemary, cypress, and eucalyptus. Taking a bath with two cups Epsom salts and one tablespoon baking soda is a powerful aura cleanser, and the drawing-out effects of the salt echo Pluto's drawing-out action.

Channel Your Intensity into Something Vital

The Pluto square can bring waves of intensity and sometimes bouts of obsession. Even if you've never had trouble sleeping, you might find yourself waking up at night with circular thinking. The key is to channel this energy, focus, and drive into something meaningful. The intensity and obsession that can accompany your Pluto square are great for research, writing, or anything that requires your total focus. Be aware that you may at times seem to be a little over the top for others now. This will pass, and you will feel grounded again, but in the meantime, try to be self-aware and mindful, because not everyone is in the same headspace as you. If you are obsessing over a lost love, even your best friend might eventually reach their limit after the fifteenth midnight call in which you need to go over every minute detail of the relationship. If this is the case, find a good therapist to take some of the edge off it for your friend. You still need to process. Journaling and sacred creative expression can be immensely therapeutic for channeling intense feelings or obsessive thinking.

Journal Reflections for Your Pluto Square

As you reflect on your own narrative at this threshold, contemplate the following:

- What patterns do you find yourself repeating that you'd like to stop?
- Do you constantly find yourself attracted to the same kinds of people or find yourself in the same situations? What does that look like?
- What do these people or situations remind you of? Can you identify a feeling that you've felt before?
- Trace this feeling back to the earliest time you can remember. What comes up?

- Do you find yourself constantly sabotaging yourself, despite your best efforts? What do you think might be behind this?
- What do you believe to be true about the world? About people? About relationships? About yourself? Name at least three things for each.
- Do you compare yourself with others? How does this serve you?

Chapter 9

A Magickal Tool Kit for Your Pluto Square

If we embrace Pluto, instead of trying in vain to fight it, it can be a potent magickal ally. We've already looked at Pluto as a powerful agent of change and facilitator of shadow work, both of which can be integral parts of magick. Call on Pluto to illuminate the hidden, to see old patterns, and to release psychological and spiritual toxins. Release and letting-go spells are intensified with the energy of Pluto. Work with Pluto to create rituals for regeneration and rebirth, drawing energy from your deepest core for self-healing. Because Hades was known as "the invisible one," you can also work with Pluto to provide a cloak of invisibility and protection while you are undergoing deep personal transformation. Pluto can be a strong ally to help you to take back your power, and rituals to reclaim sexual sovereignty as well as sex magick are Plutonian territory. Transmuting family drama can be facilitated by Pluto. Working with so-called baneful magick, such as workings for banishing, binding, and warding, is enhanced by Pluto. Psychic protection, cord cutting, and closure rituals are also amplified. See the Pluto correspondences at the end of this chapter for more ways to align with Pluto as a magickal ally.

Pathworking: Treasures in the Dark

Whether you have decided it's time to follow the call of the Great Below for personal exploration through shadow work or something has happened in your world that has brought you to a place of reckoning, you may now be in a descent. This is a profound opportunity for self-reflection. A time to recognize that which has been abandoned—the aspects of self that have been cast into shadow. It is a time for retrospection and reclaiming that which has been lost, but it is paradoxically a time to release that which no longer serves us. When we remember the parts of ourselves that we have set aside, tucked away and forgotten—we can allow those aspects of ourselves to resurface and to speak. Embarking on a descent is entering a time of deep inner work and catharsis, a time of *composting* our many layers, and doing the work of transforming the stories of our lives into the rich, dark soil that will contain new creative potential. Whatever your unique path to the underworld, witnessing, honoring, and holding yourself with compassion are the keys to surfacing and rebirth.

The following pathworking is best done at night on the waning moon or when the Moon is in Scorpio, and it is best done after dark. Find a quiet place where you will be undisturbed for about fifteen to twenty minutes and turn off your phone. Ground and center in your preferred way and clear the space by burning essential oils or incense (check the correspondences at the end of this chapter for suggestions). Wear unrestrictive clothing and get into a comfortable position. Use pillows for support if needed and a blanket to keep warm and comfortable. If challenging emotions arise during this pathworking, check in with yourself. Have a journal and a pen ready to write about the feelings that come up. Call a friend or your therapist if you are feeling overwhelmed or revisiting trauma.

You are wandering through a lush and fertile valley. The heat of the day has released the heady perfume of roses, figs, and pomegranates, and the sound of

awakening night birds fills the air. It is just beginning to cool, and Venus is disappearing in the last rays of the setting sun. You have been walking a long time when you come upon a magnificent gate. You place your palm against it, and it swings open easily on its hinges. You step inside, the shadows deepening all around you. The gate shuts behind you with an audible click. The air smells different here, like darkness and earth, and there is a hush, as if all sound has been absorbed.

The mouth of a great cave is before you. You pause and look back over your shoulder, but the world outside the gate is blanketed in shadow. A soft glow emanates from the cave, and you take a deep breath, stepping across the threshold. You realize the floor of the cave is sloping gently down, and you are descending deeper and deeper into the earth. The path you tread levels and opens into a vast chamber illuminated with the flickering light of torches. Caskets of jewels and treasure glitter in the incandescent light. In the center of the room sits a woman on a throne adorned with skulls and sheaves of dried poppies. You realize that Ereshkigal, Queen of the Underworld, sits before you. Her luminous dark eyes contain all the mysteries that have ever been. She holds out her hand and beckons you to approach. She speaks in a low and resonant voice: "What brings you to the Land of Shadow?"

You reflect for a moment. How have you come to find yourself in the underworld?

Ereshkigal speaks: "Your shadow is emerging now, because whether you realize it or not, you are now strong enough to face it, to peer behind the veil and shine a light on what was abandoned in the darkness. Hold that part of yourself with compassion, witness it without judgment, and know you are safe, you are resilient, and you are loved." Ask the wounded part of yourself if it has anything to say or what it needs from you.

Spend as long as you need dialoguing with that part of yourself that has been in shadow for so long.

Ereshkigal speaks: "There is also untold buried treasure within the dark. What have you forgotten or left behind that can help you at this crossroads?"

Again, take as long as you need to allow images or words to arise.

You awake from your reverie. Ereshkigal speaks: "Your story is not over yet.
Take what riches you have found here in the underworld and go back to the land
of the sun. May the treasures you have found in the shadow lands enrich you,
temper you, and make you wise. Go, with my blessing."

You thank the goddess and make your way up through the cave. The gate is
slightly open, and you walk back through into the land above. It is a new dawn.
The first birds are beginning to sing, the sun is coming up, and Venus is now
rising as the morning star.

Ritual: Through a Glass, Darkly

Dr. John Dee, Queen Elizabeth I's astrologer and advisor, famously
gazed into a black obsidian mirror for spirit work. This fascinating
object, among some of his other occult affects, can be viewed at the
British Museum. Scrying is the practice of gazing into a reflective
surface in order to gain insight and to see beyond the veil. Scrying
surfaces and mediums vary and include tea leaf reading, fire scrying,
cloud scrying, and of course the ubiquitous crystal ball. Although the
practice of scrying with a dark mirror is often used for divination and
spirit work, it can be an invaluable tool for shadow work. You can
find relatively inexpensive obsidian scrying mirrors at many meta-
physical shops or order one online. You can also easily craft your own
dark mirror in a variety of ways, such as painting the surface of an
old mirror black, or by simply filling a dark bowl with water. I found
an amazing art nouveau dressing table mirror in an antique shop in
Cornwall that I use for scrying. The handle is made of ebony, and it is
inlaid with beautiful silver flowers. Something about this piece called
to me, and its energy is so palpable I will confess I felt compelled
to put it away until I decided how it would be used. Eventually, I
cleansed it and charged it outside under the light of the Full Samhain

Moon in 2020. I then painted the surface black, and it has proven to be a powerful tool for reflection. I recommend hunting secondhand shops and antique stores for interesting old mirrors to use for scrying, but remember to cleanse them and consecrate them before use. Alternatively, you can scry with a smooth, dark crystal, preferably a sphere. I highly recommend black moonstone or jet for this purpose.

Don't be concerned if you don't get answers or insight for all the following questions the first time. Shadow material is buried deeply in the personal unconscious, and it is usually a process to bring it to light. It can be helpful to keep a shadow journal as you do this work and make it a practice to set aside a time each week or each month to check in with your scrying mirror. Also, don't forget that there is "gold in the shadow," and this ritual can reconnect you with aspects of yourself that you may have left behind or forgotten. Remember that much shadow material was pushed there at an early age, sometimes even at a preverbal stage. Bringing the shadow to light is the first step; the process of integrating it takes time. Be patient and remember self-compassion. If any material arises that is triggering, don't hesitate to seek support.

You may choose to set up a simple altar and include any deities, stones, colors, or other items from the Pluto correspondences starting on page 112 to enhance this work. The candles may be inscribed with the glyph for Pluto:

You may also wish to connect with one of the chthonic deities such as Ereshkigal, Persephone, or Hecate to guide you through the shadow realms. If you do choose one of these deities as a guide, be sure to familiarize yourself with their stories and myths beforehand out of respect and to align with their energy. A deity is much more inclined to lend their support if you take the time to develop a relationship with them, rather than just uttering their name while knowing nothing of who they are.

The best time to do this ritual is at night on a waning moon, or when the Moon is in Scorpio, although you can engage with it any time you feel called to engage in shadow work. Make sure you are somewhere private and quiet for at least half an hour and remember to turn off your phone.

You Will Need

- A dark surface to scry into
- Black candles (If you wish, you may inscribe them with the glyph for Pluto, protective symbols such as the pentacle, or other sigils of your choice.)
- Journal and pen

Ground and center in your preferred way. If your tradition includes casting a circle, do this before you begin. Burn herbs, essential oil, or incense to clear your space and focus your intent. Check the Pluto correspondences starting on page 112.

Light the candles. Position the mirror so it is about the same distance away as your computer usually is, unless you are using a handheld mirror. Have your journal and pen within reach. Make yourself comfortable and allow yourself to slip into a light trance state through square breathing. Breathe in for the count of four. Hold for the count of four. Exhale for the count of four. Hold for the count of four. Repeat this sequence until you feel deeply relaxed.

Keep your breathing a little slower and deeper than usual, allow your vision to soften (eyes half closed and slightly off focus), and gaze into the mirror.

Say,

> *Mirror dark, grant me sight*
> *Of shadow hidden from the light*
> *The buried fragments of my soul*
> *I call back now to make me whole*

Allow any impressions to arise. They could be symbols, images, words. Don't censor what comes up, don't try and force it, and let the images change as they will. When you are ready, ask the following questions as you gaze into the mirror, being sure to give ample time to receive answers. Engage in dialogue with whatever comes up, a practice Jung called *active imagination*. You can ask, *Where do you come from? How did you once serve me? What do you need from me?* Perhaps the most important part of this work is the act of witnessing the fear, pain, rage, grief, and limiting self-beliefs that reside in your shadow.

Ask, *What is hidden?*

Ask, *What do I fear?*

Ask, *What blocks my path?*

Ask, *What lies beneath my fear, rage, envy, grief? What early memories arise?*

Ask, *How does my shadow emerge? How has it served me? How does it sabotage me?*

Ask, *How do I recover the lost fragments of my Self?*

Ask, *What treasures have I left behind that it is now time to reclaim?*

You can pause between questions to write down any impressions, or you can wait until you are done. Some work best with an uninterrupted flow, while others like to jot down notes in the moment.

When you are finished, put out the candles, stretch, and turn on some low lights as you come back to waking consciousness. Read over what you have written. Some may choose to continue journaling with the material, or you can return to it before your next shadow work session. Pay attention to your dreams and notice any synchronicities that arise over the next few days.

Allies and Correspondences for the Pluto Square

STONES AND MINERALS: Amethyst, black kyanite, black moonstone, charoite, indicolite tourmaline, iolite, labradorite, phantom quartz, rhodonite, topaz

> **FOR TRANSFORMATION:** Manifestation quartz, moldavite, opal, pietersite, shattuckite

> **FOR RAGE AND RESENTMENT:** Blue lace agate, chalcedony, kunzite, peridot, thulite

> **FOR GRIEF:** Apache tear, dioptase, jet, rhodochrosite, rose quartz

> **FOR PURGING AND RELEASE:** Aquamarine, danburite, enhydro quartz, obsidian, scolecite

ESSENTIAL OILS: Patchouli, spikenard, cypress, storax, clary sage, rosemary

DEITIES: Hades, Pluto, Persephone, Inanna, Ereshkigal, Ishtar, Hel, Thanatos, Osiris, Sekhmet, Kali, Cerridwen, Mary Magdalene, Green Tara

COLORS: Vanta black, deep red

HERBS: Foxglove,* white briony,* mandrake,* damiana, woad, wormwood,* black fern (*Indicates baneful plants. These plants are highly toxic, and great care and research should be taken before working with them in any capacity, including handling them.)

PLANT ALLIES FOR SUPPORT: Saw palmetto, white pond lily, milk thistle, dandelion, turmeric, black cohosh, rue, elecampane, skullcap, ghost pipe, burdock

BACH FLOWER REMEDIES FOR SUPPORT: Cherry plum, chicory, crab apple, holly, pine, sweet chestnut, walnut, willow, vine, heather, white chestnut

SIGN: Scorpio

HOUSE: Eighth

ELEMENTS: Water, earth, fire

TAROT CARD: Death

Chapter 10

The Neptune Square
Liminal
Age 39 to 43

Neptune was discovered in 1846 and was the only planet in the solar system found by mathematical prediction as opposed to empirical observation. Its discovery coincided with the Romantic era, which embraced the concepts of emotion, beauty, intuition, nature, the sublime, the numinous, and the desire to escape to the romance of an earlier idealized time. Neptune is the Roman equivalent of Poseidon, the Greek god of the sea, and brother of Jupiter and Pluto (or Zeus and Hades from the Olympic pantheon). The sea symbolizes the unconscious and is connected to dreams, emotion, and imagination, so it is of no surprise that Neptune is considered the most ethereal of all the planets. Archetypally, it is the principle of transcendence and the desire to merge with something greater than ourselves, to return "home" to a state of fusion and belonging. It represents where we yearn for mystical experience and union with the Divine. Neptune takes approximately 164 years to move around the sun, and stays in a sign for about 14 years. It is the modern ruler of Pisces and relates to the twelfth house.

Neptune is associated with the beauty and transcendence of mysticism, religion, and devotion, as well as spiritual growth. It encompasses spiritual ecstasy, altered states of consciousness, and euphoria. The list of notable writers, poets, and artists who have embodied Neptune's divine madness is lengthy. Hildegard von Bingen and Teresa of

Ávila were medieval Catholic mystics who entered altered states of religious ecstasy and produced powerful creative works that inspire to this day. Similarly, the ecstatic writings of Sufi poets Rumi and Hafez stir the reader now as they did more than 700 years ago. Neptune is the sensation of reverence when we step inside a beautiful old church or temple. It is the sense of awe when we stand before the stones of Avebury, Stonehenge, or Newgrange. It is the feeling we get when beholding a sunset, the ocean, or a great work of art. It is the inspiration that enchants the words of poets, the artist's brush, and the musician's song. It is the elation that comes with the total immersion of falling in love. It is the compassion that moves us to tears and the desire to heal and to help. Neptune represents our connection to the Divine, the surrendering of the ego to merge with something sacred and meaningful. It is the sense of being one with all that is.

While Neptune can be a force of spiritual transcendence and beauty, like all archetypes, it has its shadow. Neptune can also distort, idealize, and deceive. The same ecstasy that we feel when falling in love can be projection or the torturous longing of unrequited love. The term *lovesick* is undeniably Neptunian, yet some of the world's most inspired works of art and music derive from this wretched state of yearning. Neptune seduces and beguiles, painting the world with the colors of dreams and building castles in the sky. A specifically Neptunian device, projection is putting the object of one's adoration on a pedestal and seeing them through proverbial rose-colored glasses. Projection is literally projecting one's idealized anima or animus onto the Other, who may or may not have some of the qualities that we idealize. In a projection, the Magical Other will never actually be all that we choose to see, as it is an idealized image that no human person can live up to. Often, they have a slight resemblance to our inner ideal, and once we recognize that, they suddenly embody our personal version of the knight in shining armor. If you're interested in learning more about projection and romantic love, I highly recommend *We: Understanding the Psychology of Romantic Love* by Robert A. Johnson.

With Neptune projections there is also often an element of the Savior or the Redeemer at play. We might find ourselves in the position of wanting to save someone, seeing their magical potential if only they would quit drinking, leave their partner, or see their own worth. On the other hand, we may be the one yearning to be saved and project the Redeemer archetype onto someone because we perceive that they might be the one to take us away from it all, get us back on track, or make everything finally okay. There is often a sense of the otherworldly in Neptunian projections—a sense of enchantment that sweeps us off our feet and for all intents and purposes carries us off to another realm. It's no wonder that so many artists, poets, writers, and musicians have found their greatest inspiration through Neptune's ethereal magic.

As Neptune is related to the spiritual, its shadow can also show up as spiritual bypassing. The term *spiritual bypassing* was coined by transpersonal psychologist John Welwood, author of *Toward a Psychology of Awakening*. Essentially, spiritual bypassing is using spiritual practices or beliefs to avoid doing the work of facing and integrating the shadow. Some examples of spiritual bypassing include the following:

- A preoccupation with "the light" at expense of the sacred dark
- Repression of one's own shadow that can lead to suppressed rage, grief, and anger (see chapter 7 for more on shadow work)
- Leaning on empty platitudes: e.g., "Everything happens for a reason," "Karma will take care it," and "I guess it was just not meant to be."
- False compassion
- The idea of being of service at the expense of one's own well-being
- The desire to be *seen* as compassionate or "in service" rather than actually doing something tangible to create change or help in a meaningful way

- Excessively idealistic and refusing to look at reality
- Automatically posting "thoughts and prayers" on social media in respect to a tragedy without truly witnessing the situation or helping in any real way
- Repeating and reposting new age/pseudo-psychological buzzwords without context or meaning
- Not going deep enough into a practice or belief to understand it on a meaningful level
- Appropriating parts of a belief or practice for their aesthetic value and social media potential

Neptune moved into its own sign, Pisces, in February 2012, where it will be until 2025, when it will move into Aries. Since then, thanks to the internet, all things spiritual have been in the spotlight like never before—including those things that have the *illusion* of being spiritual. And while this focus on the spiritual has brought new ideas to the masses and enabled sincere students and worthy teachers to find each other, Neptune in Pisces most certainly also has manifested in its shadow side. Remember that the shadow of Neptune can be expressed in deception and idealism. Neptune distorts and beguiles, and if we don't keep our feet, it can lead us down the proverbial garden path, at best offering up empty theatrics and buzzwords, as well as self-styled spiritual teachers whose greatest contribution may be that they are social-media savvy. And of course, Neptune also rules glamour, so what you see is not necessarily what is.

Apart from showing up as spiritual bypassing, Neptune's shadow can be even more insidious. Neptune also encompasses delusion and blind faith. The shadow of Neptune is behind fundamental religion, false gurus, and charismatic leaders. Neptune's shadow can also manifest as addiction and substance misuse. If there are any commonalities beneath these expressions of Neptune, it is the desire to transcend our worldly concerns, the need to belong, the desire to feel a part of something greater than ourselves, and the impulse to shift personal responsibility to an outside source.

The Greek god Dionysus has many parallels with the Neptune archetype. The hedonistic nonbinary god of wine, viticulture, divine madness, religious ecstasy, and the theater, Dionysus was the original charismatic leader whose female followers, the maenads, would dance themselves into a frenzy of divine madness and intoxication to honor their god. Leaving their homes and confined roles as wives and mothers, they would roam the forests and abandon themselves to ecstasy and altered consciousness. This is comparative to those who give up their worldly possessions, identities, and even family to follow spiritual leaders who promise freedom and a sense of belonging in a new life, unencumbered by the expectations and burdens of their former roles. Part of this new life usually includes the heady sense of abdicating all responsibility and accountability for the self to the group and its leader. Interestingly, one of Dionysus's epithets was *Eleutherios*, meaning "the liberator."

One of the attractions to giving up one's sense of self is a return to childhood, or more specifically a return to the womb. In *The Astrological Neptune and the Quest for Redemption*, Liz Greene explains, "Such a return occurs at death, and in the throes of mystical experience, and in the twilight world of the drug-induced trance. It can also happen whenever primal emotions rise up and flood consciousness, so that the 'I' disappears. This can, at certain times and for certain people, seem delicious and full of enchantment, particularly if life is cold, harsh, and frustrating."[55] Being birthed into the world is, in a sense, like being cast from a primal state of fused oneness and bliss and into earthly reality with all its attendant suffering. Neptune's shadow encompasses the longing to transcend the bonds of reality, whether it be through addiction, substance misuse, spiritual bypassing, or another one of the myriad paths to illusory freedom through oblivion.

Because a difficult Neptune transit can coincide with the desire to escape, it often heralds an existential or spiritual crisis. We may feel a

---

55. Liz Greene, *The Astrological Neptune and the Quest for Redemption* (York Beach, ME: Weiser, 1996), 5.

loss of focus or footing and temporarily be drawn into a state of dissatisfaction and an overwhelming feeling of separateness or isolation. There may be an inexplicable longing to go "home" or return to a time or place (real or imaginary) where one felt safe. This can be accompanied by a pervasive sense of meaninglessness and depression. We may yearn for something we cannot name, a sort of spiritual malaise settles upon us, and we lose ourselves in reverie and contemplation. We need to realize that these times have a purpose. As uncomfortable as they can be, they are the urgings of the soul and a call to a more meaningful way of life.

The Neptune Square

Neptune makes a square aspect to itself in our birth chart at some point between the ages of 39 and 43. This is the second midlife transit, and it often overlaps with the upcoming Uranus opposition. Occasionally, it also overlaps with the tail end of the Pluto square. Once it begins, this transit usually lasts about a year and half, slipping off and on the exact degree in your chart as it moves backward and forward through its retrograde and direct motion.

Although all the crossroads transits are by nature liminal times, perhaps the one that most aligns with the concept of liminality is the Neptune square. Like Inanna hanging on the hook, the Neptune square is often a time when all we can do is surrender. The hook is the equivalent of the crucifixion, the stasis before resurrection. It represents the death of the ego and a suspension from our usual waking consciousness. It is the dark before the dawn and the feeling of powerlessness when we are plunged into our internal world, cast adrift and lost in the abyss. It is a time to let go of our desire to control, go within, and yield to this necessary step in our individuation. And although we might feel submerged or stuck for a time, we must keep faith that the path forward to new life begins with acceptance and the recognition that we are more than our ego selves—and there can be wisdom in waiting.

This rite of passage reminds us that we are not out of the woods yet. Although the Pluto square likely brought us to the underworld in some way, it also brought us face-to-face with our shadow, and we are now invited to find meaning in what emerged from the depths. People often experience a sense of ennui and dissatisfaction with the lives they've built to this point. We may experience intense anxiety and existential angst during this passage, but there is a deeper purpose to it. Astrologer and author Clare Martin explains, "In our culture we do not recognize or value the natural ebb and flow of the soul's engagement with our lives, with all its joys and sufferings.... We are forced to turn inwards, no matter how painful that may be, and in that process, to meet our deeper selves."[56] Although the Neptune square can be a time of intense soul searching and self-questioning, at its heart it is a call to a more spiritual and meaningful life.

One of the first things we may notice as we get closer to the Neptune square is a loss of focus. We might feel that we've lost the path we've been on, or feel a sense of separation from who we used to be. Any glamour we have connected to our sense of self can be stripped away during this transit. Feeling stranded far from familiar shores, separated from our former sense of self, sad for no apparent reason, or mourning those things that did not come to pass is common now. We might experience spells of intense longing, yearning for something we might not even be able to name. Ruminating over our accomplishments is common during the Neptune square. We might be grieving over lives we didn't live, choices we didn't make, or things we wanted to do that have not come to fruition. The realization dawns on us that although we are not old, we are no longer young. We may struggle as we come to terms with the awareness that some of our dreams will not likely come to pass. Dreams and treasured fantasies we've carried since our youth can dissolve before our eyes during the Neptune square. Perhaps we had aspirations of being a famous musician, a prima ballerina, or a professional athlete. We know now that some

---

56. Martin, *Alchemy*, 89.

of our dreams are not grounded in reality. And although there is still time to create fertile new dreams to aspire to, there is usually some grieving for the things that we know we will not realistically achieve.

We also feel more sensitive during the Neptune square. We may find ourselves crying more than usual. Any barriers to the suffering of others we have erected in emotional self-defense dissipate. Even if we never considered ourselves an "empath" before, we are now suddenly tuned in to the suffering of the world and we can't seem to turn it off. It's important to limit consumption of news and other types of media, including films with themes of violence or injustice so we don't become emotionally overwhelmed or revisit trauma. I'm not saying to bury your head in the sand by any means, but being conscious of how much you're emotionally affected by outside sources is just good self-care. It's also helpful to make space for intentional solitude and learn techniques to ground and center, as well as to clear any energy that belongs to others.

Depression and anxiety tend to surface around this time for many reasons. Remember that one of the manifestations of Neptune's shadow is escapism. Because we can feel so sensitive and porous during this transit, it's tempting to want to reach for something that will just make us feel (even temporarily) better. We may feel the urge to escape from uncertainty, the unknown, or our own insecurities. Neptune can be both seductive and deceptive. A glass of wine (or whatever your poison/medicine) can be okay, but if you find yourself reaching for that glass more and more often, check in with yourself. The same goes for prescription drugs like sleeping pills, anxiety medication, and antidepressants. Neptune and substance misuse go hand in hand. Of course, talk to your doctor to make any decisions regarding medication, but be your own best advocate when it comes to your health, and do your research. What begins as something to just get you through the night can quickly become a dependency during this time.

Escapism can take other forms besides substances. Neptune's action inspires us to want to blur the edges, soften the harshness, and retreat to a world of fantasy. For some it's drugs and alcohol;

for others it's food and binge-watching Netflix. Even though it is not easy to keep your balance during a Neptune time, the trick is to try to be as awake and conscious as possible. Granted, the Midlife Transits can bring up some difficult issues to grapple with, and we are all human. Divorce; the end of a relationship; kids leaving the nest; wondering how long you'll be single; losing your job, your sense of self, and your youth—the list of possible stressors at midlife is a long one.

Deception is another theme that can arise now, and it can manifest in several ways. We may be deceiving ourselves by refusing to listen to our intuition about a situation or a relationship. A peculiar thing seems to happen during Neptune times—our intuition is heightened, and we may be more tuned in than ever through dreams, hunches, and feelings in our gut. However, we may be inclined to disregard these messages from our intuition, preferring instead to see what we want to see and believe what we want to believe. It's not uncommon during the Neptune square to press the snooze button on what we know to be intuitively right. We might disregard red flags, that nagging feeling in the pit of our stomach, and be inclined to give someone the benefit of the doubt, even though in our secret heart we know the truth of a matter. This can be in a relationship, at work, or in any other life area. Trust your gut and summon the courage to check out your intuitive inklings. It may be tempting to allow everything to just keep going along as is—Neptune encourages us to avoid conflict or hard edges—but you will be happier in the long run if you seek clarity rather than hiding your head in the sand.

On the other hand, we might be the ones doing the deceiving. This might be unconscious. Keeping secrets during this time is highly inadvisable, as they tend to come out now. We may convince ourselves that whatever we're keeping secret is for the best. Although there are many kinds of secrets, most are toxic and in the long run poison our relationships with others and with ourselves. Interestingly, I have found that for those whose Neptune square overlaps with their Uranus opposition, secrets can come out in an unexpected and dramatic way. Of course, like every transit, we may project shadow elements onto others in our life, and the big reveal might come from someone else.

Manipulation, blurred boundaries, and passive-aggression can arise now. Once again, it's important to connect with your intuition and to any feelings arising in the body that may be alerting us to emotional manipulation or when our boundaries are being overstepped. Emotional manipulation is a ploy to get more control or power in a relationship, and it can be hard to detect. However, we usually have an awareness that something feels off. We might begin to doubt ourselves and our perceptions. We may feel off balance without understanding why. We might start to feel that we are losing ourselves in the relationship and that our self-worth is impacted. These relationships can be damaging to our self-esteem and are psychologically toxic and destructive. If you find yourself in a manipulative relationship, it's important that you seek help, as it can be difficult to see clearly, disentangle, and take your power back.

On the other hand, as hard as it may be to admit, or even to see in ourselves, we may be the one engaging in manipulation. It takes a lot of self-awareness and humility to acknowledge that we may not be perfect, and sometimes it is easier to accept being a victim than own that we may be using manipulation to keep the upper hand. Manipulation is often connected to passive-aggression. Check in with yourself: Do you communicate your needs clearly? Do you expect others to anticipate your needs, and then get angry, retaliate, or withhold if they don't? Do you see yourself as the long-suffering victim of more powerful others? Are you always doing for others and secretly resenting them for it? Do you receive secondary gains by identifying with the Martyr archetype (i.e., receiving approval by being perceived as helpful, understanding, self-sacrificing etc.)? Do you believe deep down that others owe you something for all that you do? Can you detect an ongoing pattern in your life of somehow always ending up the scapegoat, doormat, or pushover? Be as honest with yourself as you can. Some get a false sense of power by identifying with the Victim archetype. I have observed that those who resort to manipulation or chronic passive-aggression as an interpersonal relationship pattern have been deeply hurt, abandoned, or neglected at some point in the past and have yet to resolve this trauma. Somewhere along the line they have learned that the only way to get their needs met is covertly. To the extent that they have felt powerless, the internal impulse is to regain a sense of power and control, but in an indirect way. Until they shine a light on these blind spots, they will continue to re-wound themselves and others without understanding why. This is a signifi-cant opportunity for shadow work and would probably benefit from outside therapeutic perspective. During the Neptune square, these undercurrents may arise to be examined so we can live with more clarity about our own motives and those of others.

Because this rite of passage can be associated with the dissolution of the ego, we must be alert to becoming overly passive and impres-sionable. Things can go two ways. If we have always been in control of our life, we may now feel the temptation to give up some of that control, and allow ourselves to be swept away, shifting responsibility outside ourselves, and relaxing the tight reigns we've held on our-selves and our lives. On the other hand, for those who have planned their lives down to the last detail, the tidal wave of Neptune energy can be overwhelming and frightening. But the irony is that the more we try to control situations unfolding in our lives at this time, the more difficult and unwieldy things can become. To an extent, we need to learn to surrender and go with the flow. Paradoxically, we also need to be mindful of just how far we allow ourselves to let go. There's an inclination to be more gullible now that we are not seeing people or situations clearly. It's not the best time to make commitments of any kind, romantic, financial, or other, as you may be seeing what you want to see, rather than what actually is.

Whether we are married, in a committed relationship, or single, we may be entranced and captivated by someone who seems too good to be true. We can easily find ourselves in over our head, consumed by our projections and immersed in a fantasy world. Clients have described this state using words like, "I've never felt like this before," "This is the one," or, "I just know we've been together in another lifetime." Those are Neptune words. We are more easily seduced, metaphorically and literally, during this transit. Neptune can act like a love potion, and there can be a heady, intoxicating aspect to our attractions. Neptune love stories are the kind of thing we read about in fairy tales. They often feel epic and archetypal. Usually, they have some element of longing and embody the "star-crossed lovers" theme in some way. She lives in England. He's married. Whatever the obstacle, it heightens the romance, as well as the sense of urgency, the longing, and the pining for the other. We have never felt so alive, so much truly ourselves, so *seen*! We may feel we have stepped between the pages of a storybook and cannot eat, sleep, or think of anything else but the object of our desire. Neptune love stories are the height of romance, and for all that they are not usually viable in the real world, you will likely never forget your time in that enchanted realm.

All of this is not to say that one can't find the love of their life during their Neptune square (I did), but it is important to allow the projection to wear off before making any long-term commitments, and you have truly gotten to know one another, warts and all. Real love is not only mutual attraction, but kindness, respect, and a willingness to work through the ups and downs that come with a relationship over time. If you do end up spellbound by a Neptunian romance, enjoy it for all it's worth, but be prepared for a wake-up call when the spell breaks. I can guarantee that not everything is quite as it seems, and you will discover a few truths that are not immediately apparent. The question is, will those truths be deal breakers or things you are both committed to working on together as a team? Only time will tell.

Neptune teaches us the medicine of letting go. The late author and astrologer Howard Sasportas writes, "No matter how hard we try, our attempts to maintain the status quo fail. *It is only when we finally do give up and let go that we create the possibility for something to come along and help us through our difficulties and into our next step or phase of life.*"[57] Although tears will likely flow, and for a time we may feel washed up on an unknown shore, this threshold is an opportunity to bring more meaning into our lives. This rite of passage may humble us, and our hearts might break, but they will also break open, making space for more love, wisdom, compassion, and depth. Throughout this rite of passage, you will also likely experience moments of numinous inspiration and unparalleled beauty. Despite the challenges, we are given the chance to embrace a sense of enchantment and experience the magic that comes through letting go and leaning into a deep and transcendent sense of connection with the sacred.

---

57. Sasportas, *The Gods of Change*, 101. Sasportas's italics.

Chapter 11

Navigating Your Neptune Square

As challenging as this rite of passage can seem, its purpose is to dissolve the ego self we have constructed and to connect us to something greater. By letting go of old identities and ways of being in the world, we surrender to spirit and make space for alternative perspectives. We are searching for meaning in our lives at this juncture, and while some find solace and meaning in returning to the teachings of the faith they were brought up in, others look further afield for inspiration.

Cultivate a Relationship with the Spiritual

Wherever you are drawn, the Neptune square is a powerful time to reclaim a spirituality on your own terms. Spirituality is very personal and unique to everyone, so use this time to cultivate your own experience with the sacred. Although I have clients who identify with a particular spiritual path, there are many who are just beginning to hear the call to connect with their spiritual selves. These clients usually want to know where they can begin, what they should read, and what to watch out for. The spiritual choices and directions in the world today are more varied and confusing than ever before. As I have mentioned, we are especially impressionable during a Neptune time. We can easily be drawn to the seductive call of Dionysus in its many guises. Watch for anything or anyone that seems too good to be true. Although this is a time of seeking and inspiration, *cultivate spiritual discernment*. Be social media savvy and don't get drawn in by buzzwords or glamour. Do your research: How long has a teacher/public figure been practicing? Who were their teachers or influences? Have they written any books or blogs? Do they say anything of substance? Do they make bold claims or rely on flash to sell their brand? Do they seem grounded and clear in the presentation of their work? What feeling do you get when you go to their pages? Do you feel calm, interested, comforted, or inspired? Or do you detect ego and thinly disguised sales pitches? Don't base the merits of a spiritual teacher by the number of followers they have on Instagram—they might just be good at playing the game.

Begin a Meditation Practice

Meditation is especially beneficial now. There are many different kinds of meditation, but even if you can find ten minutes a day, perhaps in the morning before you begin your day or in the evening when you have some quiet time, simply focusing on the breath will help you calm and center. There are many great meditation teachers to tune in to. I am partial to Jack Kornfield's, Tara Brach's, and Pema Chödrön's works. Do a YouTube search to find one who works for you and begin.

Ground and Center

Because Neptune transits dissolve existing structures, keep your grip and be conscious of maintaining healthy boundaries. If you feel yourself being pulled into a sense of the surreal or engulfed by waters over your head, it is important to have a practice to ground and center. There are many techniques for grounding and centering, but this is one I have used for years. Begin by sitting or lying down. Feel the tangible solidity of ground, earth, or floor beneath you. Do a few cycles of square breathing: breathe in for the count of four, hold for the count of four, breathe out for the count of four, and hold for the count of four. Repeat until you feel a sense of calm. It's also helpful to have a touchstone that keeps you attached to the here and now that you use whenever you do this exercise. It can be a special crystal, a piece of jewelry, a stone—something you can hold in your hand that keeps you rooted in the tangible present. I have a black tourmaline wand, about four inches long, that I've used for this purpose for many years. I also keep it on my table when working with clients and occasionally pick it up to help bring me back to center. Apart from the association of black tourmaline being grounding and protective, I have held it so many times that the moment I pick it up, it acts as a prompt that lets my deeper self know that it's time to ground.

Release What Doesn't Belong to You

We can be exceptionally tuned in during Neptune times, which can be both a blessing and a curse. On one hand, we are often more intuitive and psychic than ever. On the other, we may be soaking up the energies of others without even realizing it. Some symptoms of taking on too much energy from others include feeling tired, cranky, anxious, body aches, sad for no apparent reason, and a sense of heaviness, as well as receiving thoughts, dreams, and impressions that don't seem to belong to you. It's important to get some intentional solitude, such as a walk in nature, to help get some space and differentiate between what's yours and what belongs to someone else. Regularly clear your home and workspace with cleansing and protective herbs. My favorite is a mix of cedar, yarrow, and mugwort, which I craft from the plants in my witches' garden and the trees on my property. You can easily find these powerful plant allies in a natural food store or online. You can either take the dried herbs and sprinkle them onto heated charcoal in a burner made for this purpose or create a bundle that you can light.

Spend Time Near or in Water

Because Neptune is associated with water, it can help you step into the flow, connect, or release by heading down to your local body of water. Ocean, lakes, rivers, and creeks all work well. If you live near a well, it can be an immensely therapeutic and magical way to connect with water, as well as being a portal between the unseen realms, or the otherworld and the world above. Head down to your local pool and swim or relax in the hot tub. Ritual baths are also a great way to connect with the water element and work with Neptune's medicine.

Take Care of the Essentials

There is often a distinct lack of clarity during the Neptune square that can filter into any area of your life. Neptune times can be confusing, foggy, and uncertain. It is all too tempting to just let things slide and avoid the everyday drudgery of the outside world. Part of Neptune's process is to help you let go, but most of us have responsibilities to ourselves, our families, and our jobs, and we can't just phone it in and tell people that they'll find us on our meditation pillow or in the bath for the next year and a half. Although it is not usually advisable to make big commitments during this transit, it is important to take care of the essentials. Like Ninshubur in the Inanna myth, we need to access that part of ourselves that takes care of the practical details of our life while we are doing deep inner work.

Lists will be your best friend during this transit. Whether you write out your to-do list on paper, put in your phone, or have it on your computer, keep your lists where you easily see them. Make sure to check off things you've tended to, and keep the list updated. Don't overwhelm yourself by putting too much on the list, and do create more than one for specific activities if it helps. Put the most import-ant tasks down first, like bill payments and health-related appoint-ments, such as checkups. You can create lists for health, groceries, books you'd like to read, and appointments. Lists will help you keep on top of things through this nebulous time and ensure that you don't space on the important things. Don't be hard on yourself if you can't do all the things. If you make lists and check things off, you'll feel a sense of increased clarity and focus, two commodities that can be hard to come by now. Do make sure you take care of the important things, but if you slip once in a while, be gentle with yourself and begin with one item. It will make a difference and provide you with a sense of accomplishment that encourages you to check off more items on your list.

Take Small Steps as You Enter the Unknown

A Neptune transit is a little like entering the land of Faery. Nothing is quite what it seems, and we can be dazzled by illusion. Slow down, and don't try to get to the other side all at once. It is a process that will last for approximately a year and a half. So please be patient with your progress. Give yourself permission to take small steps, as you tend to your inner life. Try not to put too much on your plate if you are feeling overwhelmed, and do not feel guilty for not doing enough. Remind yourself that you are enough just as you are. This is a liminal time in life and must be honored as sacred space.

Forgive Yourself

It's common now to look back on the trajectory of our lives and wonder why we did or did not do certain things. However, berating yourself for choices made or not made is a waste of time. Choice is subjective and complicated, influenced by numerous factors, including our shadow, early conditioning or trauma, and where we were in our lives at the time we made a specific choice. Acknowledge the past, but don't allow yourself to become mired in self-blame or guilt, which can prevent you from moving on. Making mistakes is how we learn. Self-forgiveness is not condoning or disregarding actions and choices we are not proud of, but owning them and then releasing them so we can move forward. Remember that everything we don't accept within ourselves gets pushed into the shadow, and that includes guilt, shame, and self-reproach.

We are not born with wisdom but accrue it by learning from our experiences, allowing our engagement with the world to temper us. Remember that everyone makes mistakes and has regrets, we are human and in a constant process of evolving and learning how to navigate life. Treat yourself with as much kindness, empathy, and understanding as you would a good friend. Make amends where necessary and write down all that you learned from the choices you made or didn't make. Reflect on what you've learned and how far you've come.

Embrace Self-Love and Self-Acceptance

The Neptune square is a powerful opportunity to embrace self-love and move toward self-acceptance. It's important to recognize that self-love is not the same as self-indulgence. Self-love is consciously choosing to honor your own needs and make choices that support your well-being on all levels. Self-love helps you choose healthier and more supportive relationships, take care of yourself, and get more joy out of life. Loving yourself is essential for taking care of others. If you are constantly negating your own needs to take care of other people, you will burn out, become resentful, and eventually have nothing of real value left to give. Depending on early conditioning, self-love might just sound like a vague concept that is difficult to connect with. If this is true for you, there are things you can do to begin cultivating more self-love in your life.

Begin with taking a good look at the people in your life. It's important that you surround yourself with community and friends that you feel good around. Do your friends generally support you? Is there a good balance between give and take in your relationships? Do you feel like you can be yourself? Although it is not easy, it might be a good time for a check-in regarding who gets to share your time and your life. Toxic relationships are one of the worst enemies of a healthy sense of self-love.

Make time to do the things you enjoy. If you've forgotten what your passions are because you're burned out looking after others, it's time to do an inventory. Think back to what you used to like and write it down. Add anything you're curious about trying and write that down too. If you need supplies or anything specific to engage in the things you love (e.g., art supplies), it is an act of true self-love to go out and get the things you need. This sends a clear message to your subconscious that your desires, passions, and interests are important. Prioritize your time so you can make space for what you enjoy. Even if you can carve out just a few minutes a day, it's a beginning, and it will do wonders for your self-esteem and your stress level.

Take a look at your surroundings. The simple act of tidying up your home and workspace is a strong message to your subconscious self that your immediate environment matters, and therefore so do you. Take some time to make your space beautiful, charming, and special. Pick some flowers and put them on your desk. Create an altar. Make your bed. Burn your favorite incense. Fill your home with beauty, intention, and things that are meaningful to you. The same goes for your self-image and how you show up in the world. Put your best foot forward. Do an inventory of your wardrobe, and give to charity anything that is worn, the wrong size, or no longer in sync with who you are becoming. Take some extra time to dress with intention before you leave the house. Even if you work from home, putting a little extra attention toward your appearance is a form of magick. I've worked at home for seven years, and I often dress for the magick I want to conjure when I'm writing, teaching, or seeing clients online. My clothes, my hair, and my jewelry are all magickal talismans that help focus my intent. Remember, Neptune is about glamour, which is not always a bad thing.

Make a list of everything you appreciate about yourself. Go back to when you were growing up and work forward until now. What stands out for you? What qualities do you have that you would admire if they were in someone else? What do you love and appreciate about your body? What about you are you grateful for?

Ask for help when you need it. Self-love is about respecting your limits and not being afraid to ask for help when necessary. Dull the voice of the inner critic that says you are not worthy or loveable if you can't do it all on your own. The inner critic is a liar. We all need help from time to time, and far from being a sign of weakness, it is a sign of valuing yourself enough to recognize when you need a hand. It's also a great way to collaborate. If you've built your self-image on never asking for help, doing everything yourself, and taking care of everyone's needs but your own, the ironic thing is no one likes or respects you more for it. There is literally no payoff.

Practice good self-care: get enough sleep, exercise, eat well, and take care of your health. When you take care of yourself, it has the effect of boosting your self-esteem, because the message is *you are worth the effort*. Another benefit of good self-care is an overall sense of increased well-being. Just getting enough sleep and regular exercise brings countless benefits, including improved mood, better immune system, increased energy, reduced risk of heart disease and stroke, sharper focus and memory, regulated body weight, and potentially longer life. Self-care equals self-love.

Whether you're comparing yourself to friends or strangers on social media, one of the worst enemies of self-love is comparing yourself with others. Remember, you cannot see behind the scenes. Even if it appears that your friends have the best marriage or the most noteworthy accomplishments, sometimes not all is that it seems. Nothing and no one is perfect, and to compare your precious life and unique sacred story with *appearances* is not kind to yourself or realistic. This especially goes for strangers on social media who appear to have it all. You simply have no idea what the interior of their life is like. Social media is a particular kind of beast that has cultivated comparison like never before in history—a carefully curated façade of persona. Further, marketing is a skillset. Influencers and celebrities have help so they can achieve the look of the lifestyle they're selling: professional photographers, editors, assistants, and so on. To compare your actual life to the visage created by professional lifestyle experts is just unfair.

Accepting yourself as you are and acknowledging that you are enough is the cornerstone to self-love.

Trust That This Too Shall Pass

This rite of passage can be a time when we feel our most vulnerable. No matter how bleak the circumstances, sometimes the best thing to do is to remind yourself that this too shall pass. The nature of life is change, and if you are experiencing a low point, you will not always feel the way you do right now. Be good to yourself, practice good self-care, and reframe your self-talk in a way that lifts and supports you rather than tears you down. This juncture is part of the sacred story that is your life, and you are the protagonist of this story. Try to see this chapter through an archetypal lens.

Journal Reflections for Your Neptune Square

As you reflect on your own narrative at this threshold, contemplate the following:

- What is naturally ebbing in your life at this time?
- What are you carrying that belongs to someone else?
- What does your intuition tell you?
- Are you disregarding your gut feelings to avoid an unpleasant truth?
- Are you receiving secondary gains by identifying with the Victim/Martyr archetype?

- Do you have a pattern of ending up the doormat, pushover, or scapegoat? What undercurrents do you think keep this pattern in play?
- What does spirituality mean to you?
- What does self-acceptance mean to you?
- If you practiced more self-love, what would that look like?

Chapter 12

A Magickal Tool Kit for Your Neptune Square

If we work willingly with Neptune's medicine, it can be a powerful transpersonal magickal ally that opens subtle dimensions. Call on Neptune to help heal old wounds, summon compassion for yourself and others, and transcend the everyday. Work with Neptune's magick to develop your intuition. Working through ancestral patterns and connecting to those who have gone before, as well as access to the otherworld, are facilitated. Work with past lives and engage with spirit work. Align with Neptune to set magickal intent for casting a glamour, trancework, and shape-shifting. Working with the water element is naturally amplified by Neptune, and spells that involve the ocean, lakes, wells, rain, and bath magick are amplified. Healing work of all kinds is intensified by Neptune. As Neptune is sometimes referred to as the higher octave of Venus, sacred creative endeavors are complemented by its otherworldly magic. Pathworkings, dreamwork, automatic writing, and spirit journeys are all under Neptune's domain.

Chapter 12

Pathworking: Letting Go
with Ocean Medicine

Living at the water's edge in the Pacific Northwest, I am blessed to behold the ever-changing moods of the sea on a daily basis. Neptune's connection with the ocean is poetry containing hidden messages about letting go and allowing change. Connecting with the soul of the sea, even if you live in a desert, is a powerful metaphor for navigating the threshold that is the Neptune square.

The following pathworking can be done at any time you need to let go. Find a quiet place where you will be undisturbed for about fifteen to twenty minutes and turn off your phone. Ground and center in your preferred way and clear the space by burning essential oils or incense (check the correspondences at the end of this chapter for suggestions). Wear unrestrictive clothing and get into a comfortable position. Use pillows for support if needed and a blanket to keep warm and comfortable. If challenging emotions arise during this pathworking, check in with yourself. Have a journal and a pen ready to write about the feelings that come up.

You are walking through a deep cedar forest. The fog is low, and the mist is a living thing, encircling the roots of trees. You can scarcely see your feet as you make your way along the path. Overhead, a raven's hoarse voice sounds, and you inhale the deep green scent of the woods. You are carrying a small bundle that is becoming a little heavy, and you want to sit down and rest for a while. Suddenly, you realize that you are standing before the same Douglas fir with gnarled roots that you could have sworn you already passed. The ghostly fog is like a shroud of gauze, and it is impossible to see what direction you are moving in. You are in a landscape of swirling mists and the path is not straightforward. You realize that you are lost and pause for a moment trying to get your bearings. With your sense of sight obscured by the fog, you close your eyes and tune in to your other senses and ways of knowing. Somewhere not too far off, you hear the

rhythmic sound of the ocean meeting the shore, and you follow the measured cadence.

You come out of the woods onto a vast stretch of sand. The increasing strength of sunlight through the fog becomes a brilliant white light that envelops the sea, and the mountains beyond are hidden from view. You hear the sound of small waves gently lapping the shore, and breathe deeply the scent of salt and sand. You sit on a sun-bleached driftwood log, and a few feet away a small fire crackles, encircled with stones. You open the bundle you've been carrying. Inside are things you know it's time to let go of. You might find grief, old wounds and identities, or relationships that no longer serve you. You reach deep into the bundle and, one by one, take out those things you've been carrying that have become so heavy. Allow these things to assume a shape or a symbol, and gently take each from your bundle and acknowledge it, honoring it as a part of your story. Lay each on the sand at your feet. When you have completely emptied the bundle, you rise and take these things to the little fire, reverently giving them over to the blaze. You watch as the flames catch, transforming the things of the past into soft gray ash. Carefully, you bend and scoop up the ashes and carry them to the water's edge. You wade in, the water is warmer than you expected, and the white light is blazing now as the sun begins to burn its way through the fog. Allow the water to hold you safely, like a womb. You cup your hands and blow the ashes into the sea. The ebbing tide scatters them and pulls them farther and farther away from you, until they disappear. If you have tears to shed, allow them to flow freely and become part of the ocean. The dazzling fog is lifting now, revealing brilliant patches of blue sky and the clear outline of the mountains beyond. The sun on the water sparkles like a thousand diamonds, creating opalescent prisms. You wade further into the warm, enveloping water and gently bathe your face and hair, feeling the soothing, life-giving waters cleanse away the past, renewing you as you prepare to move into the next chapter of your story.

Ritual: Softening the Edges

Neptune is often associated with the desire to escape and blur the edges, particularly when we are feeling raw, emotional, or over-whelmed. And while the dangers of unhealthy escapism are obvious, there are other, more constructive ways to escape that can be a healing respite. Like the tides, our lives are cyclic, moving out and moving in. It is wise to respect this natural ebb and flow and to give ourselves permission to retreat when it is time. We must learn the art of tending ourselves and honoring our rhythms.

As Neptune rules the ocean and water, bath magick is a natural fit as a conduit for its ethereal energy. Ritual bathing for purification, healing, renewal, and other therapeutic uses has featured throughout the ages in many cultures, from the public baths of ancient Rome to the bathhouses of feudal Japan. Immersion in water for ceremonial purposes is seen in Christian baptism, the ritual purification in Arabic culture known as *ghusl*, and the Jewish ritual practice *mikveh*. Because Neptune times can bring with them the need for amplified self-compassion and self-love, a bathing ritual can be just the medicine required to step away from the harshness of everyday reality, if only temporarily while you nurture yourself and gather your strength. This ritual is best done at night on a Full Moon or when the Moon is in Pisces, although it can be done anytime you feel the need to retreat.

You Will Need

- White candles
- Music (something relaxing; I suggest *Returning* by Jennifer Berezan)
- Herbs, essential oils, or incense for consecrating the space
- Neptune Dream Tea (see page 144)
- Bathrobe
- 2 cups Epsom salts or Himalayan pink salt

- 1 tablespoon baking soda
- 12–24 drops of essential oils of your choice (check the correspondences for suggestions)
- Recording or audio version of the pathworking starting on page 140 (optional)
- Journal and pen

Create your sacred space: clean your bathroom first, including your tub, using natural cleaning products, before you begin. Leave your devices out of the room, and make sure your ringer is turned off. Dim the lights, light the candles, and put on the music. Burn herbs, essential oils, or incense to clear and consecrate the space, and if you wish, set up a small altar near the tub, referring to pages 145 and 146 for correspondences. Place water and a cup of Neptune Dream Tea on the altar or near the tub. Ground and center in your preferred way. If possible, take a shower first to cleanse yourself before the bath. Visualize letting go of any spiritual, emotional, or physical toxins that need to be released. Watch these things leaving your heart, your psyche, and your body and being easily and effortlessly washed down the drain. Remember that tears are cleansing too, and if you have any to shed, let them flow.

After you shower, dry off, put on your robe, and begin filling the tub. Add the salt, baking soda, and your chosen essential oils. I recommend rose and lavender for self-love, opening the heart, and relaxation. Check the temperature as it fills and adjust as needed. While you are waiting for the tub to fill, make yourself comfortable and take the cup of Neptune Dream Tea in your hands.

Say,

By ocean shore and moonlit sea
I release the past and wander free
Safe and sound within the dream
I slip inside, betwixt, between

Raise the cup to your lips and take a sip. Drink the tea slowly. Taste all its complexity and allow yourself to align with the plant spirits within the herbs. Notice any images or impressions that arise. When the tub is full, set a gentle timer for 20 to 30 minutes and slip inside. Breathe deeply and slowly and feel whatever ails you melt away. Give yourself permission to drop down into a state of deep relaxation. If it feels right, this can be a good time to do the pathworking from this chapter beginning on page 140. Either record yourself reading it (in this case, you'll need your phone, but be sure to turn the ringer off), or listen to it on the audio version of this book. Whether you decide to journey with the pathworking or prefer to have this time to allow your own visions and dreams to arise, take this time to step away from everyday reality and bring gentleness and healing to any parts that need it.

After 20 to 30 minutes, get out of the tub and slip into your bathrobe. Take some time to journal what came up for you. Keep the lights low, and if you leave the bathroom to journal in another room, take the candles with you to extend the feeling of soothing tranquility. Your dreams may be more vivid and more lucid than usual tonight.

Neptune Dream Tea

You Will Need

- 1 part skullcap
- 1 part rose petals
- 1 part lavender
- 1 part mugwort
- Tea strainer or muslin teabag

Mix the dried herbs and petals together and place 1 to 2 tablespoons into the strainer or cloth teabag. Place in a tea mug. Heat water until it comes to a boil and pour it over the herbs until covered. Let it steep from 15 minutes to 1 hour. Note: the longer mugwort steeps, the more potent (and bitter) it becomes. Taste after 15 minutes and adjust the timing. If it is too strong, you can add some honey to taste.

Allies and Correspondences for the Neptune Square

STONES AND MINERALS: Ajoite, aquamarine, cavansite, chalcedony, enhydro quartz, larimar, lepidolite, opal, pink tourmaline, smithsonite

FOR LETTING GO: Chrysocolla, chrysoprase, dioptase, smoky quartz, watermelon tourmaline

FOR MEDITATION AND CONTEMPLATION: Ametrine, celestite, iolite, rainbow moonstone, tanzanite

FOR SOOTHING SADNESS AND ROUGH EDGES: Blue topaz, blue lace agate, morganite, prehnite, rose quartz

ESSENTIAL OILS: Jasmine, sandalwood, lemon balm, ylang-ylang, spearmint, lotus, lavender, rose

DEITIES: Neptune, Poseidon, Dionysus, Sedna, White Tara, Kwan Yin, Oshun, Yemaya, the leanan sidhe, Mami Wata, Melusine

COLORS: Celedon, teal, azure, silver-green, emerald, aqua, slate, silver, gray

HERBS: Mugwort, lobelia, jasmine, wild lettuce, marsh mallow, lotus, ocean plants such as seaweed, poppy,* psilocybin,* cannabis,* ayahuasca* (*Indicates plants that may or may not be legal in your area)

PLANT ALLIES FOR SUPPORT: Lemon balm, schisandra, rhodiola, ashwagandha, rosemary, peppermint, holy basil, hawthorn, chamomile

BACH FLOWER REMEDIES FOR SUPPORT: Centaury, cerato, oak, clematis, gentian, honeysuckle, larch, red chestnut, wild oat, wild rose

SIGN: Pisces

HOUSE: Twelfth

ELEMENT: Water

TAROT CARD: The High Priestess

Chapter 13

The Uranus Opposition
Awakening
Age 41 to 45

Uranus was discovered unexpectedly in 1781 by Sir William Herschel and has the distinction of being the first planet to be discovered with a telescope. Although it had been observed before, it was not recognized as a planet and was thought to be a star. The discovery of Uranus as a planet turned the prevailing worldview upside down and disrupted the status quo. Until its discovery, it was accepted that the solar system contained seven planets that ended with Saturn, the furthest planet that can be seen without a telescope. The discovery of Uranus was a wild card, an unexpected consciousness-expanding event that forever changed how we see our universe. Its discovery also coincided with the Age of Enlightenment, also known as the Age of Reason, a time in Europe that challenged tradition and championed science and reason over the old order of faith, religion, and superstition. It also heralded the separation of church and state, as well as the ideals of liberty, brotherhood, and individual freedom. Astrologer and author Howard Sasportas explains, "Right from the start, Uranus was a rule breaker, with little regard for the traditional cosmological scheme. And, as synchronicity would have it, Uranus timed its entrance with flair, to coincide with three major social revolutions also intent on disrupting the established order of things."[58]

---

58. Sasportas, *The Gods of Change*, 28.

And, ever since its discovery, Uranus has indeed been connected to change, rebellion, and awakening. Uranus is named for the Greek sky god Ouranos, the father of Kronos (Saturn), and is the only planet with a Greek name instead of a Roman name. Ouranos was also the grandfather of Zeus (Jupiter). Ouranos was one of the primordial gods of ancient Greece—Father Sky—and although there is not much written of him or his exploits, he represents the remote, separate, abstract, and lofty ideals that have come to be associated with the astrological Uranus and the sign it rules, Aquarius.

Unusual in its rotation, Uranus is tilted so far that it appears to orbit the sun on its side. It also rotates in a retrograde direction, opposite the direction that most other planets turn (besides Venus), and has completely different seasonal changes than the other planets. Uranus spends approximately 7 years in each astrological sign and takes roughly 84 years to orbit the sun. Uranus is the modern ruler of Aquarius and associated with the eleventh house.

Often referred to in astrology as the Great Awakener, Uranus represents the principles of liberation and individuation. Uranus is associated with social change and breaking the rules of whatever came before. It also rules science and technology, the future, community, independence, and change. Like its unique rotation and different seasonal patterns, Uranus has also come to be associated with the unconventional, the idiosyncratic, and the unusual. Uranus is seen as a visionary outsider, bringing new ideas to the collective and resonating with the ideals of social justice.

Significant Uranus transits reflect the Tower in the tarot, depicted in the Rider-Waite Tarot (and many other decks) as a tower struck by a sudden bolt of lightning. The top of the tower is blown off, and a crown is thrust up into the air. Flames shoot out of the windows and people fall from the tower headfirst with expressions of shock and panic. This is the action of Uranus, disrupting the status quo and existing structures (as symbolized by the crown). Uranus is also associated with surprise, shock, upheaval, crisis, and sudden unexpected change or catastrophe. The Tower also hints at the liberation and freedom that comes with the overthrow of antiquated systems.

In what has filtered into common astrological thought but may have been originally introduced by Richard Tarnas in his book *Cosmos and Psyche: Intimations of a New World View,* Uranus has been archetypally compared to the Titan god Prometheus. Humans did not possess fire, mathematics, science, medicine, and agriculture, as these attributes were thought to be the privileged province of the gods themselves. Prometheus tricks the gods and steals fire as well as the other godly possessions and gives them to humankind. He is then punished by Zeus, who chains him to a rock, as an eagle eats his liver for eternity. Eventually, however, Prometheus (and his liver) is saved by the hero Heracles. The myth of Prometheus embodies the spirit of Uranus, as it illustrates the overthrow of the old order to better humankind through progress and breakthroughs that come through rebellion and breaking the rules. Tarnas writes that Uranian themes are "reflected in the myth of Prometheus with striking poetic exactitude: the initiation of radical change, the passion for freedom, the defiance of authority, the act of cosmic rebellion against a universal structure to free humanity of bondage, the urge to transcend limitation, [and] the creative impulse."[59]

When we experience a major transit of Uranus, we often undergo a time of abrupt personal change, upheaval, and crisis, usually followed by the emergence of new ways of thinking and being in the world. Parts of us that were previously undeveloped suddenly surface, changing the status quo in our own lives and sometimes in our closest relationships. The energy of Uranus is edgy, electric, and sudden, like a lightning bolt out of the blue, and significant Uranus transits are commonly accompanied by feelings of intense restlessness, agitation, and anxiety. Uranus is the part of us that wants to expand, emerge, develop, or tear it all down like the Tower so something new

---

59. Richard Tarnas, *Cosmos and Psyche: Initiations of a New World View* (New York: Plume, 2006), 94.

can be born. Anything or anyone that we perceive to be holding us back or limiting us in any way can be pushed aside as we move toward freedom and the wholeness of individuation.

On the other hand, we might be projecting our inner need for change on the people in our lives. Subconsciously, we may know we are not growing in a particular career or relationship, when suddenly our partner decides to leave or we lose our job. One of the adages of Uranus is "expect the unexpected," and during a significant Uranus transit, things do seem to happen out of the blue. But in hindsight, we can often see the lead up to events that perhaps we were ignoring, so great was our fear of change. If we work with our inner Uranian impulse toward evolution and incorporate small changes as we approach a Uranus transit, it can act like homeopathic medicine. In homeopathy, the guiding principle is "like cures like" or "the principle of similars." Our psyche needs change during these times, and if we give it change in small doses, it will not become stagnant. This is *propitiating the gods*—honoring that part of our psyche that is aligned with a particular archetypal force. You will still experience your Uranus transit, but its effects may not seem to be coming from out of the blue and might not be so disruptive, as we have acted consciously on our own behalf, making appropriate offerings to the gods within.

The function of Uranus in the psyche is to break us out of ruts we've fallen into. In many ways, Saturn is the antithesis of Uranus. Saturn represents the established order, while Uranus represents new awareness that precipitates change. Saturn certainly has its place, and we can't do much of any consequence without it, but too much identification with Saturn leads to apathy and lack of growth. During Uranus times, our higher self conspires with the universe to break through those places in our psyche and in our lives that are closed off. Saturn wants to keep everything as is, while Uranus knows that way lies paralysis and the death of the soul. Uranus times can coincide with crisis and disruption, but they usually also lead to authenticity and new life.

The Uranus Opposition

As it takes Uranus 84 years to revolve around the sun and come back to its natal position, at some point between the ages of approximately 41 and 45, Uranus will oppose its position in your natal chart by sign and degree. This is your *Uranus opposition*, and it is widely considered to be the transit that most closely coincides with what society has deemed the midlife crisis. As mentioned in the last chapter, the Uranus opposition can sometimes overlap with the Neptune square and also the upcoming Saturn opposition. It is usually a turning point, a sudden crossroads that can destabilize the status quo in our lives, but is often followed by liberation and individuation.

The themes of quickening and awakening that are often experienced during the Uranus opposition echo Inanna's return to life in the underworld. Whatever is keeping us stuck begins to shift. And as we shall see, while the action of Uranus is often unpredictable and disruptive, it is sometimes just what we need to wake up and renew our engagement with the world and our deeper selves. We emerge reanimated from our stasis and reclaim our potency. We thirst for freedom, to express ourselves authentically, and to affirm that we are alive. Like Inanna, we might awaken to find that we too have been in an underworld of sorts. And even if the wake-up call has been disruptive, we feel a sense of edgy excitement that calls us back to life. The Uranus opposition is often a turning point in our narrative.

Much like Uranus's unexpected discovery that shook the entire worldview of Western civilization, the Uranus opposition can herald something new exploding into our awareness that shakes the foundation of our lives. This can be an inner revelation that rocks us to our core or an event that in one fell swoop challenges what we believe to be true about ourselves, our relationships, or the world we live in. Often this discovery comes as a shock, and some things may never be the same. Like the Tower, the Uranus opposition can strip away the veils of illusion, exposing the truth, which can be intensely inconvenient and overwhelming. To the extent that we cling to our beliefs and illusions about reality, we are often left raw and quaking after such a revelation. Some liken the explosive nature of the Uranus opposition to the classic so-called nervous breakdown; we may feel stretched to the limit, like we're falling apart, or simply numb and vibrating. Although not everyone comes to this juncture in such a dramatic fashion, if you do find yourself in this place, it's important that you sit with your wounded parts and hold yourself with compassion. You may be in emotional shock, and it's imperative that you treat yourself with kindness and seek support.

So what can possibly shake us so violently that we are left in shock at this threshold, our cherished beliefs shattered? Having worked with hundreds of clients at this crossroads, I have been privy to the ways that this transit can manifest. Some find out that their partner has been hiding a sex addiction. Others discover that their spouse is planning to leave them. Some have found out that longtime friends have shockingly different politics and values. I have worked with several mothers who find out during this time that their child is struggling with substance misuse. A few clients were diagnosed with an illness during their Uranus opposition. And others are suddenly and unexpectedly let go from jobs that they've held for years. Like every transit, the Uranus opposition will play out in a unique way depending on our birth chart and the specifics of our lives, but it will always carry the same archetypal themes of discovery, revelation, destabilization, and the opportunity to find meaning in the truth that has been revealed.

Regardless of how your Uranus opposition plays out, even if it manifests in a less dramatic way, it is common to feel anxious, restless, and uneasy. It is natural to feel "wired," edgy, and jittery, and insomnia is not unusual during this rite of passage. You may find it hard to focus and be more distracted and scattered than usual. You might find it more difficult to control your emotions and might react in unusual or unpredictable ways. Friends, family, and colleagues might wonder why you are acting out of character. It's not unusual to make seemingly out-of-the-blue decisions that surprise the people in your life during this transit.

If you are reading this and see this transit on your immediate horizon, take heart. It is not always so extreme, but it can be. I try not to sugarcoat the kinds of hard lessons that can come up at various life passages, because sometimes life can be hard, and with Uranus, it can be unpredictable. However, I find that the more conscious one can be about the underlying purpose of a given transit, the easier it can be to navigate. Remember that Uranus is that part of our psyche whose job it is to disrupt whatever is keeping us from growing. As you approach your Uranus opposition, take a good, hard look at your life and ask yourself what needs to change. How can you bring more movement, growth, and new life into your world? Significant Uranus transits are by nature unpredictable. You can look at your chart and see the house (life area) it's happening in, look at other transits happening around the same time, take your life specifics into account, and check with your intuition, and still Uranus can surprise you in the way it manifests. But you do know when you can expect the unexpected. And knowing that can be helpful.

Although the Uranus opposition can certainly be experienced as an outer force and a disruptive influence, it can also be felt as a profound inner shift that nevertheless can change our world and our place in it. Many who come to this threshold have spent the greater part of their adult life establishing a career, raising a family, or both. When they reach this stage, they may begin to question where earlier idealized versions of themselves have gone. There can be a feeling of desperation in trying to hold on to lost youth, to resurrect those old ideals. Sometimes this is when we see the stereotypical midlife crisis come into play. We feel a thirst for freedom, to rebel, to do things our way, and reclaim a sense of aliveness. If we are not conscious of the true meaning of the feelings that arise now, we may feel the urge to follow what provides an illusory path to liberty by getting out of Dodge and calling it a day on the life we've built. Anything that we perceive to be holding us back or limiting our freedom can be pushed aside, as we reach for anything that helps us feel young just a little longer: the ubiquitous sportscar or an exciting new lover. But if we succumb to these pitfalls, we're missing the point. The point is individuation. The point is breaking out of our tried and true ways of doing things and freeing up aspects of ourselves in a meaningful way so we can get on the path we are meant to be on. And while that *might* mean extricating ourselves from a marriage in which neither of us is growing or quitting our day job to travel the world, it is important to be mindful with our choices now.

Conversely, depending on our attitude toward change, the Uranus opposition can be one of the most enlivening times in our entire life. It can herald a profound change in life direction that enables us to embrace our purpose and reinvent ourselves in a conscious way. We may finally feel liberated from limiting self-beliefs or the need for external approval as we reclaim a sense of renewed authenticity and self-actualization. Unexpected opportunities can show up in the least likely places, and doors can open that usher us into a new life we could not even imagine before. Creative breakthroughs and life-changing epiphanies may bring us to a new sense of self. Life is infused with new purpose, and we are in the frame of mind to embrace it with open arms. Even if we have gone through some of the more challenging aspects of this transit, this shift can pave the way for quantum leaps and accelerated personal evolution. We are refreshed, restored, and more awake than we have been in a long time. We must remember that the lightning bolt that strikes the Tower and topples old forms also brings revelation in its wake.

Chapter 14

Navigating Your Uranus Opposition

If your life has become stuck in rigid patterns and you deny your own intuition, needs, and opinions, it's time to check in with yourself. What do you really think? What do you want? What choice will make you feel more alive? As new parts of your consciousness begin to spontaneously emerge, how can you honor yourself as a unique being with ideas of your own? Try giving yourself permission to express yourself in new and unprecedented ways with small actions at first. This will help prevent the possibility of an explosion and its unpleasant aftereffects. If you consistently reign yourself in, especially in small and seemingly inconsequential ways, the Uranian impulse can erupt, threatening structures in your life that are still viable.

Get Some Space

The effect of the Uranus square often makes us feel controlled, confined, and restrained, whether or not that is actually the case. Make sure you find time to yourself. If you can, try to arrange for time away from work and family responsibilities, even for a short while. You need room to breathe, to think, and to see who you are without the weight of the structures you've built in your life. Think of this as preventative medicine. Even just an afternoon to yourself, a night out with friends, or a weekend retreat can be helpful.

Try Something New

Whether you realize it or not, your psyche needs change at this time. This is the perfect opportunity to try something you have never done before. Whatever calls you, be mindful and avoid extreme risks. Although some risk-taking is healthy and expected during this transit, it's important to remember that due to the potentially explosive nature of Uranus, it's not a good time for throwing caution entirely to the wind.

Try On a New Persona

There's a hilarious scene in the film *Anger Management* in which Jack Nicholson's character, a famous psychologist, asks Adam Sandler's character, "Who *are* you?" For every answer Sandler provides, Nicholson rejects it, saying, "Dave, I don't want you to tell us what you do; I want you to tell us who you are." Finally, Sandler becomes visibly agitated, proving that perhaps he needs anger management after all. It's a very funny scene, but it's interesting because we do tend to identify ourselves defined by our roles. During the Uranus opposition, we might find ourselves asking the same question, and if all we can come up with are job titles and various roles we've settled into playing, we may also feel frustrated. Perhaps we didn't consciously choose our roles but fell into them by a perfect storm of circumstance. Maybe our identity is built on the expectations of others and through the lenses of the people in our life. This transit is an interesting opportunity to reflect on who you are and also who you are becoming. Who are we underneath the roles we play? It's not uncommon for people to suddenly and dramatically change their hair, style, or appearance around this time as they experiment with different aspects of who they are and how they want to show up. This is a great time for play and experimentation. The Uranus opposition is an exciting time to give voice to any aspects of ourselves that have been previously undeveloped or dormant.

Expand Your Social Circle

Again, this transit impels us to want to check out life on the other side. We might be wondering what we've been missing outside our usual sphere, or maybe we're cultivating new aspects of who we are and are curious, experimental, and searching for new perspectives at this time. This is an opportune moment to meet and mingle with those from other walks of life, with different interests. One of the easiest ways to do this is to try something new. Get out of your comfort zone and take a class, attend a meeting, or go to another part of town that you've never explored.

Let Go of the Need to Control

For those who need everything planned, sorted, and scheduled down to the last detail, this is often the most difficult of the Midlife Transits. Because of the unpredictable nature of Uranus, the status quo is often disrupted. If you meet an exciting someone, it's best not to commit quite yet. Resist the need to label the relationship and allow it to take its course. It is possible that in time it will become a long-term, committed relationship, but with Uranus, one never knows. This goes double for leaving your partner for someone new or hoping they'll leave their partner for you. Uranus energy is electric, edgy, and exciting—it can knock us sideways. But do not try to control the outcome. Relationships undertaken now can fizzle just as abruptly as they began. The bottom line is to go with the flow and resist the urge to control.

Get Grounded

I mentioned the importance of getting grounded and centered in the previous chapter because the Neptune square tends to blur boundaries, but it is just as imperative during the Uranus opposition for other reasons. And remember, these two transits often overlap, causing a real need to find your center. Earlier in this chapter, you learned that some of the common manifestations of this transit can include feelings of restlessness, agitation, insomnia, and high levels of anxiety. In certain situations, this transit can even be connected to symptoms of emotional shock. So the need to find a grounding and centering practice that works for you is critical. Meditation and yoga can be highly therapeutic right now because of their capacity to help you find a sense of calm and come back to center.

Understand Emotional Shock

Occasionally the Uranus opposition can coincide with events that precipitate emotional or psychological shock. This can happen for a variety of reasons: perhaps you found out some traumatic news, you witnessed something, or someone has broken up with you. Emotional shock ensues when the body receives a jolt of adrenaline, which activates the flight, fight, or freeze reaction that is our body's way of protecting us from the threat of danger. Symptoms can include feeling outside your body, lightheaded, like you are floating, numb, unfocused, or disconnected. Your hands may feel tingly or fluttery. Your heart might beat faster. You may feel clammy or sweaty, or you may become nauseous and may even vomit. It might feel like everything has taken on a surreal quality. Your breathing may become rapid and shallow, leading to hyperventilation. You may not be able to think straight. Emotional shock can last for a few minutes, hours, or days (or even weeks or months, when it becomes PTSD). Sometimes we have a delayed reaction and are seemingly fine in the moment, but we feel emotional for no apparent reason long after the incident that caused the shock in the first place. Emotional shock may be exacerbated if you have experienced past trauma that gets retriggered by the event.

With emotional shock, the first thing to do is try and focus on your breathing. Hyperventilation makes you feel worse, and although it is typically not dangerous in itself, it can produce feelings of lightheadedness and floating, which can be alarming. Try to slow your breathing, and breathe in through your nose and out through your mouth.

Take several drops of the Bach flower essence Rescue Remedy to help you calm yourself. When you are ready, try to talk to someone and tell them what happened. Keep warm and try to be in a calm, non-stimulating environment if possible. The extreme physiological sensations will pass, but don't hesitate to get support from a counselor or a therapist afterward.

Take Care of Your Nervous System and Adrenals

As mentioned before, whether or not you have experienced an emotionally traumatic event, the Uranus opposition often coincides with feelings of restlessness, agitation, and insomnia. It is also common for people to report feeling adrenal fatigue. It can be helpful to reduce your caffeine intake and avoid stimulants such as sugar. Keep your blood sugar on an even keel by eating nutritious small meals throughout the day, don't skip meals, and keep well hydrated. Make sure you get enough sleep, and if you are having trouble sleeping, consider exploring herbs and other plant allies. Herbs that support the nervous system, calm anxiety, and promote sleep are called *nervines* and include skullcap, wood betony, valerian, vervain, chamomile, hops, and passionflower. *Adaptogens* are herbs and mushrooms that can help balance the body and relieve mental, emotional, and physical stress. They can be taken as a daily tonic in tea. They include American ginseng, *Rhodiola rosea*, eleuthero, schisandra, ashwagandha, holy basil, reishi, lion's mane, and cordyceps. They are readily available in natural food stores or to order online. Consult an herbalist if you are unsure of dosage and for more information. It can also be beneficial to take a vitamin B supplement, including vitamins B5, B6, and B12. Magnesium taken before bed can also be a potent natural sleep aid. Massage and other types of bodywork can also help reduce anxiety and benefit stress levels in a variety of ways.

Don't Be Hasty

Although you may be feeling an overwhelming desire to go for it, whatever it happens to be, slow down and check in with yourself. You may feel excitable, champing at the bit, and ready to roll, but before you make any life-altering decisions, press the pause button and evaluate the situation as mindfully as you can. It can also be helpful to talk things over with a trusted friend, therapist, or other professional, depending on what you are contemplating.

Study Astrology

Uranus rules astrology! This can be a great opportunity to dive into a study of this fascinating path to self-knowledge. Not only will it fulfill your need to do something new and exciting, but it may help you understand the changes you are going through. Find a reputable astrologer, read their reviews, and see if they offer any classes or workshops.

Become a Social Justice Activist

Uranus rules revolution, rebellion, and disrupting the status quo. It is the archetype connected to social justice and activism of all kinds. Channel some of that energy into anti-oppression work that benefits those who are less privileged. Educate yourself about racial injustice, Black Lives Matter, reconciliation for indigenous peoples, climate change, violence against women, homelessness, addiction, mental illness, trans people's rights, and sex workers' rights. There are many ways to get involved and no shortage of opportunities to help dismantle the old guard and pave the way for a more balanced, kinder, and just world for all. Don't forget that there's more to do than share memes on social media. Hands-on work like volunteering at a shelter is important work that is sometimes overlooked. During my Uranus opposition, I volunteered for several sex worker advocacy groups in Vancouver's notorious downtown eastside, which, though often challenging, was an eye-opening perspective on the intersection of race, class, and gender, as well as on the lives of those who face multiple barriers.

Journal Reflections for Your Uranus Opposition

- What do you know in your heart of hearts needs to shift?
- Where are you feeling stuck in a rut? What is blocked or stagnant?
- What have you always wanted to try?
- What parts of yourself have been repressed or invalidated that you would like to reclaim?
- What is one small change you can make now that will "propitiate the gods"?
- Describe who you are underneath your usual roles or job title.
- What would be different in your life if you were self-actualized?
- If you could reinvent yourself, what would that look like?
- If you have discovered an uncomfortable truth, how are you taking care of yourself? What change do you think is trying to come through via this information?

Chapter 15

A Magickal Tool Kit for Your Uranus Opposition

Although Uranus medicine can be sudden and destabilizing, working consciously with it can help create necessary change, facilitate breaking with outworn tradition, and clear space for personal growth. Call on Uranus if you need to think outside the box, invite spontaneity, and create new paradigms. Direct the energy of Uranus for freedom from self-limiting beliefs and patterns, to change career direction, or when you need to take a different approach. Embrace Uranus to get out of a rut. Spells to enhance individuation and for evolving to your next level are strengthened by Uranus. Re-evaluate your goals and align with your life purpose. As Uranus is the higher octave of Mercury, work magick for communication. Align with Uranus for anti-oppression work, social justice, and resistance. Uranus also enhances magick for the community, the collective, covens, and groups. Work with the air element and storm magick. Charge magickal objects. Anything that involves innovation, trying new things, experimentation, inspiration, and improving elements of your life falls into the realm of Uranus magick.

Pathworking: The Calm in the Storm

It is no secret that the world is a more stressful place than it has been for most of us in recent memory. The pandemic, unprecedented change, uncertainty in our daily lives, social isolation, climate crisis, global instability, gun violence, access to healthcare, human rights

163

and political upheaval are just a few examples of stressors that effect everyone to varying degrees. It is also of note that people of color are disproportionately affected by stress due to structural inequality and systemic racism. An overload of sensory input and constant bombardment of news (real and fake) from our technological devices has us on edge, as we wake up and end our days in front of our screens. On top of the outside stress of living during this time, some of us are going through personal upheaval as we find ourselves at midlife, with all the attendant change and existential angst that can accompany it. The Uranus opposition is a time that often brings uncertainty, and without occasional refuge from the storm, we can feel unfocused, emotional, and scattered. At the same time, we might also begin to numb ourselves from the unrelenting assault on our senses and well-being. We long for respite and a place where we can feel safe, sound and centered.

When I lived in England, during the late 90s, I became enchanted with hedgerows, which are a ubiquitous feature of the British countryside. In Devon, some of the oldest hedgerows are over 800 years old. Hedgerows mark boundaries, offer shelter for wildlife, and protect crops by acting as a windbreak. They are a living threshold dividing one place from another and for generations have been woven with countless threads of folklore. Plants commonly found in English hedgerows each have their own lore, and include blackthorn, elder, hawthorn, and hazel, among others. Blackthorn and elder are both known as witches' trees, and each is associated with magick as well as protection, while hawthorn is a faery tree thought to mark the gateway to the land of the otherworld. In some magick traditions "riding the hedge," or "jumping the hedge" can mean traveling to the otherworld to attend the witches' sabbat or a spirit journey involving altered states of consciousness. I have always personally associated hedgerows with protection and magick, a liminal place between the worlds. I consider myself beyond lucky to have a hedgerow on my property, and when I feel the need for solitude, I spend time secreted within the hollow of its sheltering trees and brambles, invisible to the world, and whatever the weather I am protected from the elements.

The following pathworking can be done on any moon phase and at any time of the day you need it. Find a quiet place where you will be undisturbed for about fifteen to twenty minutes and turn off your phone. Ground and center in your preferred way and clear the space by burning essential oils or incense (check the correspondences at the end of this chapter for suggestions). Wear unrestrictive clothing and get into a comfortable position. Use pillows for support if needed and a blanket to keep warm and comfortable. If challenging emotions arise during this pathworking, check in with yourself. Have a journal and a pen ready to write about the feelings that come up.

You are walking along a path that meanders across the moors, passing the remains of old stone circles, the ruins of long-abandoned villages beneath the ground you walk on. The sun is beginning to set, and you have walked so far it will take hours to return to the trailhead. The quality of the light changes, and the air becomes still. The light is intense and otherworldly, and the sky transforms to a deep shade of slate, incandescent as if lit from within. Storm light. You hear a distant rumble, and moments later lightning flashes across the sky. The ethereal glow begins to fade, and the sky darkens as clouds gather in the quickening wind that rushes through the grass. A sudden crack resounds, and a fork of lightning irradiates the scene around you. The sky opens, and you find yourself caught in a violent cloudburst. You stumble forward through the torrential rain, looking for a spot to shelter from the storm. You come upon an ancient hedgerow and see an opening that is just big enough for you to slip into. Inside it is dry and protected from the howling wind beyond.

It is surprisingly more spacious inside than you imagined, and you are able to stand up. You follow a dimly lit path that winds easily through tangled hawthorn, hazel, and blackthorn. Here and there, small offerings are tucked into the brambles. It is quiet within the shelter of the hedgerow, and all sounds of the storm outside have faded away. A sense of safety envelopes you, and with every step, you leave the cares of the outside world behind. Presently, you come upon a low altar, where a single candle gently flickers. Reverently, you kneel before the altar and exhale deeply, finding yourself more centered than you have felt in a long time. You breathe in the stillness, the deep magic of this sacred place. There is an old wooden box on top of the altar. You place your hands on top of the box and close your eyes. You become aware of a deep and comforting resonance that seems to become a distant song, and while the words are just on the periphery of your perception, you realize it is the ancient voice of the spirit of the hedgerow: the sound of the trees and earth. You breathe in the resonant calm and fall into a waking dream, fully supported by the strength and protection of the timeless poetry of the land. After what seems like ages, you stir. You open the wooden box and reach inside, taking a talisman that will help guide you back to this place of peace and refuge. You stand and pay your respects and make your way back down the path and through the same portal you came in.

Outside, the sun is shining and droplets of water sparkle on every leaf. The storm has passed. You open your hand in the dazzling sunshine to see the talisman. Take a few moments to reflect on the symbolism of what you have been gifted. As you find the path that leads back to the trailhead, you are infused with the quiet knowledge that having once found your way here, no matter what is happening in the outside world, no matter the ferocity of the storms threatening to knock you off your balance, you can always access this safe and secret place hidden between the worlds.

Ritual: Harnessing the Storm

The energy of Uranus is not unlike the wild unpredictable energy of a storm. It is the electric charge of lightning, sudden, breathtaking, and dangerous. There are many different types of lightning, including one that remains a mystery even to scientists, ball lightning, which is said to be a luminous sphere of varying sizes that occasionally appears in conjunction with a thunderstorm. There are historical accounts of ball lightning dating back to the time of the ancient Greeks, and from such diverse sources as Aleister Crowley and Tsar Nicholas II of Russia.

Although the energy of lightning aligns with Uranus, because it is so strange and bizarre, ball lightning feels especially Uranian in nature.

When we are undergoing an intense Uranus transit such as the Uranus opposition, we may find that we are literally crackling with energy. It can feel like electricity is coursing through us, causing us to feel scattered, edgy, or anxious. Inner storms rage within us, which can empower or paralyze. Embodying the energy of Uranus is not easy, but if we learn to harness, direct, and channel that energy, we can use it to break through stagnation and inner blocks. We may not be able to control this energy completely, but we can learn to work with it for self-empowerment.

Uranus is said to be the higher octave of Mercury, and the Magician in the tarot (which corresponds with Mercury) reflects the idea of focusing and directing energy to create more of what we desire. We have a great deal of energetic potential at our fingertips during Uranus transits, and the inner storms that course through us during these times can be powerful opportunities for change. The best time to do this ritual is during the waxing Moon, when the Moon is in Aquarius, or, ideally, during a storm. If you wish to create an altar, check the correspondences beginning on page 169 for suggestions.

You Will Need

- Herbs, incense, or essential oils for cleansing and consecrating
- Inkless ballpoint pen or another tip for inscribing candle
- Blue, violet, or silver candle
- A bottle or container with a lid
- Journal and pen

Cast a circle if it is part of your tradition. Burn herbs, incense, or essential oils connected to Uranus to cleanse and consecrate your sacred space. Ground and center in your preferred way. Carve the glyph for Uranus into your candle and recall that Uranus is the medicine of awakening and necessary change.

Light the candle and sit comfortably. Gaze at the flame, keeping your vision softly focused on the blue center of the fire. This is the same fire that is the spark of life, the same fire that illuminates the sun and is reflected by the moon. Breathe in for the count of four, hold for the count of four and exhale for the count of four. Repeat until you feel a sense of deeper relaxation, which may be more difficult to achieve if you are in a state of extreme agitation or anxiety. This is totally fine, so try not to be too concerned. Just allow the feelings to flow through you.

When you are ready, find the location of your amplified or anxious energy. It could be in your head, your neck, your solar plexus, or your belly. Although it may be centralized in one place, it can also be dispersed throughout your body. Visualize this energy as the same electric blue that is at the heart of the center of the flame. Note any areas that feel blocked, stuck, or frozen. Gather this electrical charge with your hands, forming a luminous sphere of electrically charged energy: a ball of lightning. Hold it in your hands out in front of you. This is pure energy that can be utilized for any purpose. Now that you have it contained and focused, you can control it. It is no longer controlling you. Say,

By lightning strike and toppled tower
I hereby gather all my power
By storm and wind and heart of fire
I focus now on my desire
Though inner storms may rage inside
My will to change is not denied

Direct some of that energy to any areas that you've noted are blocked, and see it easily moving through the block, breaking through what is calcified, stuck, or stagnant.

When you feel a sense of completion, see yourself placing the sphere into your container and close the lid. Anytime you need extra energy to direct toward a goal or to clear stuck energy, you can access it. Place the closed container on your altar.

You may feel a lessening of anxiety afterward, as you have gathered all the storm energy that has been coursing through you and contained it to be used for future magick. Journal about any impressions that arise.

Allies and Correspondences for the Uranus Opposition

STONES AND MINERALS: Apophyllite, clear topaz, Herkimer diamond, moldavite, muscovite mica, phenacite, ruby, rutilated quartz, sapphire, scapolite

FOR GROUNDING AND ANXIETY: Agate, kunzite, smoky elestial quartz, tourmalinated quartz, spinel

FOR CHANGE, EVOLUTION, INDIVIDUATION: Amethyst, blue kyanite, Lemurian quartz, papagoite, tugtupite

ESSENTIAL OILS: Cinnamon, cedar, rosemary, geranium, peppermint, benzoin, cypress

FOR ANXIETY: Lavender, chamomile, bergamot, clary sage, lemon balm

DEITIES: Ouranos, Prometheus, Lilith, Sophia, Tien-Mu

COLORS: Electric blue, violet, silver

HERBS: Kola nut, guarana, cayenne, gotu kola, *Ginkgo biloba*, horehound, ginseng, cinnamon, cedar

PLANT ALLIES FOR SUPPORT: Skullcap, wood betony, passionflower, vervain, valerian, motherwort, lemon balm, holy basil, chamomile, milky oats, hops (For more, see "Take Care of Your Nervous System and Adrenals" on page 159.)

BACH FLOWER REMEDIES FOR SUPPORT: Impatiens, rock rose, scleranthus, Star of Bethlehem, vervain, white chestnut, rock water, Rescue Remedy

SIGN: Aquarius

HOUSE: Eleventh

ELEMENT: Air

TAROT CARD: The Tower

Chapter 16

The Saturn Opposition
Discernment
Age 44 to 45

Although you may once again find yourself at a crossroads, you might be relieved to hear that this is the last of the Midlife Transits. The Saturn opposition heralds stepping into a new level of maturity. Every seven years Saturn transits itself with a hard angle—conjunction, square, or opposition—signifying both a testing time and a reality check.

The Saturn Opposition

It has been around 14 years since you went through your Saturn return at approximately age 29 or 30. At that point you likely forged the structure of your present life in some way, perhaps beginning a new career, committing to a significant relationship, or starting a family. It's time for a check-in: What's working? And, perhaps even more importantly, what isn't? If you look back to your Saturn return, you may by now see a theme unfolding for how you have structured your life, how you handle responsibility, and how willing you are to work with *what is*. Around the age of 44 or 45, Saturn opposes its place in your birth chart by sign and degree, and it can be a time of fruition or a time of reckoning. Sometimes both. Either way, you are going to have to embrace a time of hard work or take a good look at the way you've structured your life and make some important decisions. For a review of the Saturn archetype, please turn to page 49.

When Inanna is revived and exits the underworld, she finds she must make a difficult choice. She has been deepened, tempered, and matured by her time in the underworld and must distinguish between what serves her and what (or who) does not. Similarly, during the Saturn opposition, we find that we too are called to learn the lesson of discernment. The Saturn opposition brings clear perception and awareness of what matters. We may be forced to relinquish illusions that we now know do not support our continued growth. At the same time, like Inanna, we come into our true power by exercising sound judgment and making the hard choices that are required for us to be true to ourselves.

If you're experiencing blocks, obstacles, and frustrations, now is the time to listen to the messages they're bringing. Where are you in denial? Where have you entrenched self-limiting beliefs that are subconsciously structuring your everyday life? What natural consequences have resulted from the actions you have taken or not taken? The Saturn opposition will illuminate all these things and more. By now, you have already experienced the opportunity for deep shadow work during your Pluto square, learned the wisdom of letting go through your Neptune square, and discovered the necessity of change that came with your Uranus opposition. Now once again, Saturn, ever the Teacher, asks you to step up and confront the reality of who you have become. The Saturn opposition can be a profound reality check that lies between your first and second Saturn return, and it is an opportunity to live the next phase of your life with increased self-awareness. Astrologer Robert Hand writes about this juncture: "It is as if you have said to the world, 'Here is what I am.' Now, during the next fourteen years, the world will reply, 'And here are the consequences of what you are.'"[60] This rite of passage is an opportu-

---

60. Robert Hand, *Planets in Transit: Life Cycles for Living* (Atglen, PA: Whitford Press, 1976), 351.

nity to shore up the foundations of your life so that it will serve you in the most relevant way possible until your second Saturn return between the ages of 58 and 60. If we want to achieve our purpose, it is time to put in the work.

Remember that Saturn is associated with time. Approximately 14 years ago, during your first Saturn return, the concept of time likely hit home as you bid goodbye to your 20s and prepared to move into your 30s. But now instead of facing 30, 50 is not too far off on the horizon. Once again, the awareness of time becomes keenly apparent, and we are called to take stock, and look at the lives we've built with an unbiased eye. We pause and look how quickly 40 came and went, reflecting how in about the same amount of time, we will be 50 years old. If we are wise, that recognition is a wake-up call. We do the important work of determining what is meaningful and look at what needs to be released so we can move forward and build the next chapter of our lives from a place of integrity and self-realization.

We may find that it's time to make some difficult choices and adjustments so that our lives more clearly reflect who we are. If you've been in a committed partnership or marriage that is keeping you from growing, it may come to an end during this rite of passage. Conversely, if you are single or divorced, it is not uncommon to get married or enter a new and significant commitment during the Saturn opposition. It is also an opportunity to re-evaluate your career, and while some are entering a phase of mastery and success in their field, others come to this point and feel a sense of dissatisfaction or the need to accomplish something of deeper meaning. If you are happy in your work, this is often a time of taking on more responsibility, striking out on your own, or taking on a position of more authority. But the price will be hard work, increased focus, and stepping up to the plate in a new way. However, if you find yourself consistently coming up against obstacles, or feeling a sense of limitation in your work, it may be time to re-define your purpose. It is common now to retrain, retool, and commit to a new career direction. Some choose to add new dimensions related to their existing work, while others decide to do something completely different.

Whatever you choose, it will likely entail discipline, focused intent, and the ability to embrace a beginner's mind. Saturn will humble you and let you know in no uncertain terms that you have to start at the beginning. Saturn will not tolerate skipped steps or self-delusion. But if you are willing to put in the work and the effort, Saturn will also reward you accordingly. Whatever you set out to do, make sure you are committed and realistic. Anything else will result in a waste of time (there's that word again), a waste of resources, and the sobering realization that life is finite. You must have a game plan. You must do your homework and be absolutely sure that what you want to build is rooted in the tangible, not in fantasy. Crumbling at the first block, obstacle, or gatekeeper with an "I guess it's just not meant to be" attitude will spell failure to grasp Saturn's lessons and is as productive as beating your head against a brick wall for a dream that is just not realistic. One of Saturn's teachings is discernment. Saturn restricts movement, slowing things down and making any undertaking feel like work. And while you will need to cultivate the Saturn qualities of patience and perseverance, you will also need to embrace Saturn's realism and know when it is time to cut your losses.

We may feel more tired than usual and have less energy during this phase. It's important to take good care of our physical health during this transit, as our immune systems may be less effective than usual. Metabolic changes are occurring that remind us that despite our best efforts, our bodies are not as young as they used to be. Your metabolism starts to slow down in your early 40s, and aches and pains that never existed until now may begin to surface, especially those things related to aging, bones, and the structure of the body, which are all ruled by Saturn. Back pain, bursitis, and repetitive strain may start to crop up. Saturn also rules teeth, so don't put off a visit to your dentist. For some women, perimenopausal symptoms are well under way, causing hormonal changes that can be vexing. If you don't already get routine mammograms, this is a good time to talk to your doctor.

We tend to process a lot during Saturn times and need to give ourselves the space for contemplation. Situations can arise during the Saturn opposition that coincide with feelings of depression and loss. You may at times feel hopeless, discouraged, and overwhelmed with self-doubt during this phase. Although we might feel the pressure to "buck up" and get on with it, it is important that we witness this threshold as one of the sacred times in life, a necessary re-evaluation of what is truly important on our journey. It can be useful to look back and remember what was happening during your first Saturn return at 29 or 30 and your Saturn square at 36 to 37. How are your present circumstances connected to those earlier cycles of Saturn? What is Saturn trying to teach you? How do Saturn's teachings play out in the arc of your story?

By now you are becoming increasingly aware of your limits, which is a Saturnian gift that brings self-definition and helps you let go of distractions that previously clouded your vision. You have learned what is important to you, what you like, and, just as important, what you don't like. As you learn the wisdom of Saturn, you waste less time on things and relationships that don't matter in the bigger picture. You have had 14 years to practice creating healthy boundaries, and although there are likely still places that you stumble, with Saturn's guidance, you are likely more discerning about who gets to share your space and time.

The Saturn opposition calls on us to make an inventory of what serves us, and this can include jobs, relationships, limiting beliefs, and habitual patterns. Perhaps something used to serve you, but it has outlived its usefulness and has even become detrimental to your well-being and continued growth. Recall when Inanna surfaced from the underworld and had to provide a sacrifice in her stead. It was her consort Dumuzi who became the sacrifice she needed to make in order to reclaim her place as the Queen of Heaven and Earth. The question is, what do you need to release that no longer performs a viable function in your life? What is blocking you from fully stepping into your power and embracing your immanent divinity?

At the Saturn opposition, we have come to the summit of the Midlife Transits. It has taken great courage, strength, and perseverance to get here. We have undergone the fires of intense transformation and overcome challenges and obstacles as we now integrate our experiences. We are more tempered than we were before. We are earning self-respect and forging a sense of self and that will see us through our next chapter. We now come to a place where we can pause and gather strength to manifest our creative vision.

Chapter 17

Navigating Your Saturn Opposition

It's time to discern what is important to you now. You have likely changed in many ways since your Saturn return at 29 or 30. Although you committed to something important at that time, you have also lived through many experiences, which have shaped who you have become over the years. What was important then may or may not be important now, or perhaps it has shifted into new forms. Once again, it's time to take stock. Take some time for reflection, and if your priorities and goals have changed, do not consider it a failure. You have changed. In some ways you are a different person now than the 29- or 30-year old who set out all those years ago. It is normal for some things to fall away while other things take precedence in your life. It is time once again to sort the seeds.

Look Back at Your Midlife Transits

You are just wrapping up one of the most important rites of passage in your life, which began with your Pluto square. Take some time to look back. How has your story evolved and changed? What did you learn from your time at the crossroads? How have you changed? Whether or not you encountered some of the more dramatic manifestations of the Midlife Transits, you likely feel like a different person than you were before they began. What wisdom do you have now that you didn't have then? Spend some time journaling and reflecting on the last few years. This will help you focus on how you want to shape and build the next stage of your life.

Build Security

Saturn is connected to security and stability in the material world, so do something now that your future self will thank you for. Maybe you've always been security minded, and have been steadily amassing a nest egg, saving and investing wisely. If so, great. But, if you've pushed the pragmatic details aside for too long, now is your opportunity to get on it. People often come to this juncture and realize with a start how quickly time passes, and retirement age will arrive sooner than expected. It's not too late to get a retirement plan and figure out your finances. Make an appointment with your bank or a financial advisor so that when the time comes, you are prepared.

Clarify Wishful Thinking

If you are considering a new line of work, going into business for yourself, or otherwise making a big change that will potentially affect your security, do your homework. While changing one's life at this or any age certainly is possible, it is imperative to clarify whether your dreams are wishful thinking or grounded in reality. Do you have a clear picture of what your idea will require in terms of time, resources, and commitment? Is it viable? How long will it take before you start making money? Who are your clients, customers, audience? Ask yourself the tough questions. Do informational interviews and ask someone who is doing something similar about the bottom line. Whatever you decide, it may not be a good idea to invest all your savings or jeopardize your family's security during a challenging Saturn transit. Remember, Saturn favors ideas rooted in the tangible, the down to earth, the pragmatic. If you do all your due diligence and still think your idea has legs, be prepared to work hard and put in the time. It is not uncommon to begin building something of real substance now. Saturn is the planetary archetype connected to manifestation.

What Do You Need to Sacrifice?

Significant Saturn transits are often accompanied by a need to release or sacrifice something in order to move forward. Like the goddess Inanna, we have come to the point where a complete rebirth or individuation is impossible without leaving something behind that has outlived its usefulness or is keeping us from moving on. Remember that Saturn also rules endings, and while it can be painful to part with relationships, personas or things that we once held dear, you will know when the time has come because holding on becomes more painful than the letting go. Please seek support if you are grieving the end of something significant in your life and treat yourself with compassion. It may take time to heal, and it is important that you take the time you need to honor your loss.

Take Good Care of Your Physical Body

Remember that Saturn rules aging as well as our overall physical bodies. This is the perfect opportunity to create self-care rituals that will take you to your next Saturn return and beyond. Health and wellness often become an obsession around this time, and that's not a bad thing, as we begin to notice changes in our metabolism and other signs of aging. This is a great time to clean up your diet. Weight-bearing exercises, strength training, dance, and running can help stave off osteoporosis, arthritis, aches and pains, and the decrease of lean muscle mass. And of course, yoga is beneficial for anxiety, depression, deep relaxation, and stress relief. Walking can also be great exercise if you do it regularly. Learn about and incorporate herbs, acupuncture, or massage into your wellness routine. The Saturn opposition is a great time to book an appointment with a trainer or a naturopath or join a yoga class. Remember that Saturn is associated with natural consequences, and while aging is an unavoidable process given that we live inside a physical body, subsisting on a diet of wine and cheese without exercise will likely not bring the natural consequences you desire. Taking good care of ourselves can promote better quality of life, improved health, and longevity.

Celebrate Your Harvests

Let's not forget that one of Saturn's epithets is Lord of the Harvest, and this juncture can also be a time of culmination and fruition. If you have worked hard and consistently made sound decisions grounded in reality, you may experience this transit as a time of accomplishment and harvest for your past actions. If this is the case, congratulations! Take some time to acknowledge and enjoy the fruits of your labor. This can be a time when you reach a pinnacle in your career and receive a position of more authority or recognition.

Journal Reflections for Your Saturn Opposition

- What have you learned and experienced in the last 14 years (since your Saturn return)?
- Look back over your Midlife Transits. Where has your story taken you?
- Where are self-limiting beliefs subconsciously structuring your reality?
- If you are experiencing a wake-up call, what do you think is the underlying message?
- What is important to you now? What gives your life meaning?

- If you are re-evaluating your career or relationship, can you differentiate between reality and wishful thinking? Are you willing to roll up your sleeves and do the work?
- What needs to be released so you can crystallize and define your life's purpose?
- Look to the past. Is there something that you have left behind or forgotten? Is there something you need to retrieve that can guide your next steps? A reminder of who you are?

Chapter 18

A Magickal Tool Kit for Your Saturn Opposition

During your Saturn opposition, align with Saturn as a helpful magickal ally. Call on Saturn to make difficult choices, especially in situations that are colored with strong emotions. Align with Saturn to guide you through significant rites of passage, and work spells and rituals for closure and moving on. If you are changing careers, asking Saturn for guidance can help you commit to a new path, as well as clarify what is fantasy and what is a foundation that can be built on. Work with Saturn to get your finances in order. Call on Saturn for the wisdom to cultivate discernment. Saturn magick can bolster your self-discipline in starting a new wellness routine, as well as helping you stick to it. See the Saturn correspondences at the end of this chapter for more ways to work with Saturn as a magickal ally.

Pathworking: Wisdom of the Elders

As I behold the dazzling autumn leaves on the oak outside my window, I am reminded that although the seventeenth-century herbalist Nicholas Culpeper noted that oak is ruled by Jupiter, it has many associations that align with the Saturn archetype.[61] Oaks have long

---

61. Nicholas Culpeper, *Culpeper's Complete Herbal*, ed. Steven Foster (New York: Sterling, 2019), 169.

been associated with endurance, perseverance, strength, and wisdom, qualities that also come with the understanding of Saturn's role in our lives. Oaks were venerated by the Druids, and it is said that the word *Druid* itself comes from the Gaelic word for oak, *Duir*, which translates to "men of the oaks," and it is known that Druids gathered and worshipped in sacred oak groves throughout England, Wales, and Ireland.[62] In Glastonbury, England, Gog and Magog are the last two ancient oaks of what is said to have been a processional path that led to Glastonbury Tor. This oak avenue survived until 1906, when all but two were cut down for agricultural land. One of the trees that was felled at that time is said to have a trunk that measured eleven feet in diameter with 2,000 seasonal rings, which would date it at around 2,000 years old. Gog and Magog have been a beloved and sacred part of the Glastonbury landscape since that time and are known as "The Oaks of Avalon." Sadly, in 2017, Gog was set on fire. It is said the likely cause was a candle left burning at the base of the tree, a stern reminder to be careful with all outdoor rituals of any kind, especially those involving fire. Although Gog is now dead, its charred remains still exist alongside Magog. These trees have witnessed the rise and fall of countless human eras. People have gathered around them for weddings, handfastings, baby-naming ceremonies, and ritual. And of course, many have sat beneath them, whispering their prayers and stories to these ancient guardians over millennia. It is no wonder that oak medicine is connected to the timeless wisdom of the elders, another Saturn correspondence.

The following pathworking is best done at night on the waning moon or when the Moon is in Capricorn and is best done after dark. Find a quiet place where you will be undisturbed for about fifteen to twenty minutes and turn off your phone. Ground and center in your preferred way and clear the space by burning herbs, essential oils, or incense (check the correspondences for Saturn). Wear unrestrictive

---

62. "Oak Mythology and Folklore," Trees for Life, 2020, https://treesforlife
.org.uk/into-the-forest/trees-plants-animals/trees/oak/oak-mythology
-and-folklore/.

clothing and get into a comfortable position. Use pillows for support if needed and a blanket to keep warm and comfortable. If challenging emotions arise during this pathworking, check in with yourself. Have a journal and a pen ready to write about the feelings that come up.

You have climbed a long and arduous journey and find yourself at the crest of a hill. You exhale and cast a glance at the terrain behind you, hardly believing you made it through some of those craggy, perilous passages. You pause for a moment and contemplate just how far you have come. You sit comfortably on the mossy ground and lean your back against a sturdy old oak, looking out at the vista before you with its uncharted peaks and fertile valleys. You know intuitively that soon it will be time to ponder the next steps on your quest, but you have earned this moment of solitude and repose. You look up and see that others have come to this place before you, as ribbons and bits of cloth are tied in the branches, carrying blessings, prayers, and healing out on the evening breeze. Darkness falls, and feeling supported by the ancient tree, you allow your breathing to slow and turn your awareness within. You become aware of a low thrumming vibration emanating from the oak that resonates deeply in your root chakra. You realize you are hearing the subtle voice of the tree itself, a silent witness to a repository of 2,000 years of stories.

Thoughts come to you: the plans you have made and the seeds you have planted—some nurtured into being, others that you've had to allow to die on the vine. The joys you have celebrated, the sorrows and initiations that have shaken you to your core. You allow these thoughts to move through you, and you watch them float by like leaves on a stream. The images rise and fall, and you lose all track of time as one vision transforms into the next. You realize that out of these dreamlike impressions emerge the threads of story: your story. You pull your woolen cloak closer around you and silently ask, "What do I need to know for the next steps of my journey?"

Take a moment and listen. Drop down and allow words, sounds, scents, images, colors, or symbols to arise. Try not to censor anything and let the message come to you as it will. Take as long as you need to receive guidance from the spirit of the oak and know that now

185

your story too will be added to its long memory to provide guidance for others.

When you are ready, you thank the old oak for its wisdom and support. Reaching into your pocket, you take out a length of organic cloth ribbon and tie your offering in its branches. You rise and look out over the panorama before you, with its myriad possibilities, and make your way back down the hill, with new insight to navigate the next chapter of your story.

Ritual: Of Crossroads and Graveyards

Whether you experience your Saturn opposition as a time of harvest or a time of reckoning (usually a bit of both), it is a good time to temporarily seek solitude and look within. No matter what the outer circumstances are of your life, Saturn will likely create opportunities for you to pause and gather insight and strength. Remember, this is approximately the halfway mark between your first Saturn return and your second Saturn return and, as such, a potential turning point that can change the trajectory of your life. It is more than likely that you will be re-evaluating priorities and taking a good look at your life while making some serious decisions. You may in fact find yourself at a crossroads.

Recall that Saturn is associated with the limitations of the physical body, aging, and mortality. Perhaps nowhere is as poignant a reminder of the finite nature of life than a graveyard. We look at the headstones of people long passed and wonder about their lives: the stories they wove, their loves and losses, their regrets and triumphs. What they left behind as legacy. We consider that they once were as alive as we are in this moment, making decisions and choices that would shape their destiny. Visiting a graveyard can be a sobering reminder that one day we too will join the ancestors, and it can help put the details of our own lives into perspective. This ritual is best done on the waning half moon or when the Moon is in Capricorn or Scorpio.

You Will Need

- A crossroads in a graveyard
- 2–4 tealights with votive holders (depending on how many directions you are choosing between)
- Earth, stones, or fallen leaves from the crossroads
- Something to wrap each pinch of earth, stone, or leaf in
- Journal and pen
- A deck of tarot or oracle cards

First, you need to locate a graveyard of your choice. Although most cemeteries are quiet and peaceful places, it is best to find one that is especially so, so you have the privacy you need. It is common to find intersecting paths within a graveyard that form a crossroads. Find one of these that feels right for your purpose. Spend some time meditating on where you are. Take note of any nearby headstones and read the inscriptions. Imagine who these people were. Take a few moments to appreciate the nature of where you are, and reflect that one day you too will be among the number of the dead. Saturn reminds you this is simply a fact of life.

Most graveyards allow lighting candles for the dead. If this is the case in yours, place a tealight in a votive safely (to the side of the path) at each point of the crossroads. Now turn your attention to your present-day dilemmas, choices, and the decisions you may be facing. Assign each path to represent a decision you need to make or a direction you are considering.

Say,

> *By earth, oak, leaf, and bone*
> *The path before me now is shown*
> *As time goes by and seasons turn*
> *I have the wisdom to discern*

Walk to the first point on the crossroads, keeping in mind what it represents. Breathe deeply and slowly. Visualize taking that path and what it could lead to. How does it feel in your body? When you are ready, go to the next point, and envision yourself taking this path. Again, check in with yourself to see how it feels. Depending on how many choices you are currently facing, do this for each one. It might be you are deciding between two directions, or it could be up to four. At each point on the crossroads, tune in to the sounds, sights, and smells around you, and consider what they may symbolize as you ponder which path to take. Perhaps you see a crow taking flight, you hear a sudden gust of wind in the trees, or a church bell sounds. At each point, take a pinch of dirt, a small stone, or a fallen leaf and wrap it up. Put it in your pocket or bag. Keep them separate and note which path each represents.

Put out all the candles but one and pick up the candle from the path that feels the truest, even if you are still not completely decided. Take the candle to a grave that particularly calls to you and leave it burning in honor of those who have come this way before. If the weather is good, and you feel safe, find a place to sit and write about what came up for you in your journal. Alternatively, you can thank the spirits of the dead for allowing you to safely reflect in this place and go home to write.

If you are still undecided, pick up each symbol one at a time (dirt, stone, leaf) for each path and hold it. Close your eyes and ask the ancestors what you need to know about each path and pull a card. Record in your journal the name of the card and anything about the image that seems to speak to you. If you are an adept card reader, take into consideration the meaning of the card, but don't discount what you immediately notice. Perhaps your eye is drawn to a certain detail in the image. If you are new to the cards, write down any details that you notice, and look up the meaning of the card.

When you have made your decision, take the symbols of the paths not taken back to the graveyard where you found them. Keep the symbol representing your final choice on your altar until it has come to pass.

Allies and Correspondences for Saturn Times

STONES AND MINERALS: Anthracite (coal), black tourmaline, diamond, epidote, fluorite, fossilized bone, jet, obsidian, smoky quartz, stibnite

FOR GRIEF OR A BROKEN HEART: Emerald, lepidolite, peridot, rhodonite, rose quartz

FOR ENERGY: Bloodstone, carnelian, fire agate, garnet, Herkimer diamond, ruby, sunstone, zircon

ESSENTIAL OILS: Douglas fir, pine, vetiver, cypress, oakmoss

FOR UPLIFTING AND ENERGIZING: Cinnamon, ginger, bergamot, cardamom, basil, juniper, peppermint, dragon's blood, clove, spearmint, benzoin, tangerine, sweet orange, rosemary, frankincense, myrrh

DEITIES: Saturn, Kronos, Baba Yaga, Hecate, Frau Holle, An Cailleach, the Norns, the Dagda

COLORS: Black, gray

HERBS: Henbane,* datura,* wolfsbane,* monkshood,* angelica, burdock, comfrey, black hellebore, mullein, shepherd's purse, Solomon's seal, holly, witch hazel, juniper, elderberry (*Indicates baneful plants. These plants are highly toxic, and great care and research should be taken before working with them in any capacity, including handling them.)

PLANT ALLIES FOR SUPPORT: St. John's wort, lemon balm, milky oats, ginseng, *Ginkgo biloba*, schisandra berries, cordyceps, holy basil, maca, hops, eleuthero root, golden root, white oak bark

BACH FLOWER REMEDIES FOR SUPPORT: Wild oat, aspen, beech, cerato, chestnut bud, clematis, elm, gentian, hornbeam, larch, mimulus, mustard, oak, olive, rock rose

SIGNS: Capricorn, Aquarius

HOUSE: Tenth

ELEMENT: Earth

TAROT CARD: The Devil

Part 3
Full Circle

All we have to decide is what to do with the time that is given us.
J. R. R. Tolkien, *The Fellowship of the Ring*

Chapter 19

Becoming Baba Yaga

All stories are a matter of perspective, and a narrative can change when viewed through the lens of another person. If you are just coming to this book now, I suggest turning to page 33 and reading the initiatory tale of "Vasilisa the Beautiful" before reading on. The following story is connected and is told from the point of view of Baba Yaga.

My hands ache now when I gather the very plants that will make the medicine that will ease that ache. And my sight too is not what it once was. When the winter sun comes out and almost warms my bones, it is easier to see what I put in my basket. As much as I loathe to leave the comfort of my feather bed, I now rise well before dawn so I can make the most of the light. And yet, I have known this forest for so long, I could find my way in the dark. I know where to find the best mushrooms for tea and where the most potent herbs dwell. And perhaps because my sight has dimmed, I find myself as many old women do: recalling scenes of the past as vividly as though they were yesterday.

Mine is a solitary life, but it wasn't always so. Spending so much time in my own company is not a hardship, though occasionally I yearn for another soul to sit at my table and tell me of the goings on beyond these woods. But mostly, I value my solitude. I have earned the right to live as I please, and besides, I can drift in and out of the past revisiting memories of what has been an uncommonly long and full life. I can close my eyes and conjure the dear faces, now long gone, resume conversations where they left off, and relive the moments that are more valuable than any jewels. Occasionally, a memory surfaces that causes me to draw a sharp intake of breath, and I am flooded with emotions that have lost none of their original intensity. But even those recollections I hold with a certain tenderness because they are a part of my story.

I realize I am lost in reverie once again, and the light is fading. I hear the distant gallop of my horseman that means darkness will soon fall. I pick up my basket and prepare to make my way back home. It has been a long day gathering plants, and I am hungry. I climb into my mode of transportation and, rising above the trees, close my eyes in pleasure at the bracing cold wind that rushes through my hair. The waning moon has not yet risen, making the stars glitter even more brightly in the night sky.

As I arrive, I am surprised to see that there is someone standing outside my gate. A young woman, a girl really, on the cusp of womanhood. I sense rather than see her trepidation. I know my reputation in these parts, which I will not deny is based in some truth. Not the stories that circulate about the eating of human flesh—that is a fallacy. But I suppose I am what some would call a witch, and I've lived long enough to know that people tend to create stories to vilify that which they do not understand. I am also the first to admit that as I do cherish my privacy, I have been known to be short tempered, impatient, and churlish on more than a few occasions with those who have been brave enough to come to my gate. Unfortunately, with the damp cold of the season worsening the ache in my hands and the hunger rumbling in my belly, this was to be one of those occasions.

In my experience, those who come to my hut come to ask for something. Long ago, after my beloved husband died and I first made this place my home, I tried to help every seeker who came to my door. I have been a healer by trade for as long as I can remember, even before I came to this dark wood at the edge of the world. People would come for the tinctures I brewed, some yarrow to bring down their children's fevers, or coltsfoot to soothe a sore throat. Sometimes they came for advice, or a charm to help them find love. I was happy to help, as this was my calling. People would leave gifts of gratitude at my door: a chicken, a loaf of bread, and, once, a beautiful feather blanket embroidered with poppies. As the years passed and I became older, the currents in the world beyond the forest shifted. People whispered about the "witch in the wood," and rumors circulated that chilled the blood. I was now long past childbearing years, and folk traded stories of the "ugly old woman whose nose met her chin, and whose breasts touched the ground." Fewer and fewer seekers came to my door, and those who did came in desperation and rarely left gifts. Occasionally some came out of curiosity, but none came with the reverence they once did. In time, I learned to protect myself from this ignorance and walled myself in with a fence of bones that frightened all but the most desperate or curious from my door.

So, wearily, I got out of my mortar, and approached the girl. I wasn't in the mood to entertain, and I wanted nothing more than to eat my supper and crawl under the covers for an early sleep. Sometimes my reputation works in my favor, and with just a little bluster, I can easily frighten off those who dare to approach my gate. I summoned my most daunting voice and called out, "What is it you seek?" I must have made the impression I intended, for the girl flinched and stammered her reply. She told me she was sent by her stepfamily to bring fire back to their home. I knew of this family she spoke of and did not hold them in high regard.

I am still not sure why I did not walk past her and leave her standing there shivering at the gate. Perhaps I felt a flicker of compassion, or maybe she reminded me vaguely of myself at that age, balanced as she was on the edge of initiation into adulthood and the untold joys and travails it would bring. Whatever the reason, I waved her in through the gate and promised her the fire she requested, but I was not about to give it just for the asking. I have not lived this long to know nothing of the importance of reciprocity. She would have to earn it. Perhaps there was something I could impart to this young woman that would stand her in good stead for the next leg of her journey.

Weary as I was, I had the girl cook supper and serve it to me. I have become a fairly good judge of character in my old age, and as I watched her nervously moving about the kitchen, I could see that although she was quite clearly afraid of me—likely having heard the more insidious tales—she was also respectful. Idly, I mused whether this might be one to whom it would be worth passing down my knowledge. Not many young people in these times respect the old ways, and many seem to believe they can skip over the steps that lead to true wisdom. I once had a daughter I would have liked to teach the ways of the healer, but she married and left for a far distant tsardom many years ago. After I washed down my supper with a cup of wine made from last spring's elderflowers, I decided to test this young one's integrity and gave her a list of chores to be completed by the time I returned the next day. I retired immediately after supper, as my bones ached from my gathering work in the woods, and I wanted to get an early start in the morning to make the most of the light. As I drifted off, visions of the past calling me to dreamtime, I could hear the girl mumbling as if to someone, but sleep soon claimed me, and I followed it into sweet oblivion.

When I returned home from my work the following day, I was surprised to see that the girl had completed all the tasks I had laid out for her. An inkling of suspicion told me there was something here that was not quite as it seemed, but I could not put my finger on it. I decided to test her further. Not only was she to clean the hut and prepare supper again the next day, but I also gave her a chore so difficult it would be nearly impossible to complete without cunning or some manner of otherworldly assistance. But truly, sorting the seeds, making choices and discerning what will grow from what must be left behind—even when it feels impossible—is a task that one will come to again and again in this life.

When I returned home the next evening, the yard had been tidied, the floors swept, a delicious-smelling supper bubbled on the stove, and the poppy seeds and dirt were neatly separated into two piles. When I finished the sumptuous supper she had prepared, I decided the time had come for us to talk. I began the conversation by inviting her to ask if she had any questions. However, I cautioned her that to know too much too soon can make one grow old before one's time. A sudden flash of memory. I closed my eyes for a moment, and I steadied myself, returning to the present with a deep breath.

She asked about my three horsemen, my New Day, Beautiful Sun, and Deepest Night, and I explained to her in the best way I could the mysteries of the cycles of time, a difficult concept to grasp until one has lived more than a few seasons. However, she listened well and nodded her understanding. We talked long into the night, which seemed to stretch past the bounds of linear time. As the fire grew low, I asked if she had any more questions, to which she repeated my words that to know too much too soon would make one soon grow old. I chuckled to myself. She was clearly intuitive and wiser already than others of her age, which heartened me. However, I must know how she came to complete the difficult tasks I set for her. I have learned that sometimes it is best to be direct, so I came out and asked how she was able to accomplish the work. Immediately she blushed, and I saw by the rapid rise and fall of her chest that her breathing had become quicker. She hesitated and then replied falteringly that her mother's blessing helped her.

A rush of conflicting feelings came upon me unbidden. Anger, that she had tried to deceive me when I had invited her into my home. Nevertheless, I was pleased with her honesty, although she clearly feared for her life in telling me the truth. And I must confess, I also felt a slight sense of sadness that this moment marked the end of our time together. Because, whether she was aware of it or not, the time had come for her to move into the next phase of her life. She was ready to cross the threshold. I rose abruptly from the table, accidentally knocking it over. I took her by the elbow and guided her out of my hut and into the yard. Taking a glowing skull from my fence, I placed it into her hands, and sent her back to her stepfamily with the light she had come for. Her face was a mask of terror, but she clutched the skull to her breast and ran off into the woods in the direction she had come.

I stood for a long moment looking toward the forest and sighed. She would be all right. The skull would light the path, and she would find her way through the dark. After a time, I turned and went back through the gate into my hut and stoked the little fire in the grate. Sitting at the table, I poured myself a cup of kvass and closed my eyes. I recalled another girl, who on the cusp of womanhood had no idea what life would bring. How she stumbled in fear at the threshold, not knowing what she did not know. The way she trembled at each new initiation but in time learned to trust that her intuition would guide her steps. The old woman who took her in and taught her the mysteries of plant medicine, before she set out on her own and began her life in earnest. And as the years passed, the many ways life had left its mark on her, until she accrued something that might be called wisdom and, finally, even contentment. It was all so long ago, but the memories had not dimmed with time; in fact they had become brighter and more vividly colored, more valuable than any jewels.

The real mystery that lies at the heart of the tale is that Vasilisa and the Baba Yaga are inextricably connected. They are one and the same, two sides of the same coin, mirror images of the other. This mysterious paradox is echoed in other myths that feature a pair of protagonists, including Inanna and Ereshkigal, and Demeter and Persephone. Baba Yaga was once Vasilisa, the uninitiated young woman standing on the threshold of stepping into her power. And one day, Vasilisa will come to embody all the wisdom and experience that Baba Yaga has accrued in her long life. At the same time, each still carries the seed of the other within. Reflecting on how Baba Yaga came to be Baba Yaga is at the heart of the mystery of the birth, death, and rebirth cycles and of special import to those at their second Saturn return. Once again, we enter the hut of Baba Yaga, but now it is we who are on the road to becoming the wisdom keeper, the teacher, and the wise one.

Chapter 20

The Second Saturn Return
Cultivating Wisdom
Age 58 to 60

Saturn has made another full circle around the heavens and has returned to the place it was at your birth. Once again, we stand at the crossroads, but now instead of facing 30, we are on the cusp of 60. Remember that Saturn is associated with time, and once again time takes on a tangible and sobering quality during significant Saturn transits. We look back on the story of our lives to this point and see how far we have traveled. In some ways 30 may feel like yesterday. We can close our eyes and call it all to mind in the blink of an eye: a gentle touch, a conversation, the challenges, and the unexpected joys. In other ways, it may seem like a lifetime ago. By now, we have been shaped and sculpted by life. We have been tested and tempered. And whether we realize it or not, we ourselves have also made a mark upon the world, by simple virtue of loving and being loved, of adding our experiences and voice to the collective. And once again, the unknown beckons as we stand on the edge of the dark wood. We are called to reflect, to take stock and re-envision our place in the world, as we contemplate who we have become. We now carry hard-won wisdom we could not even have imagined 30 years ago as we set out on the road to creating a life. What doors did we unlock with the keys that were given us?

Chapter 20

The Second Saturn Return

The second Saturn return is a major rite of passage that marks the end of a cycle in our life and is conversely the beginning of a new and perhaps final chapter. Remember that Saturn returns to the place it was at our birth approximately every 30 years, and you will be around 90 years old the next time it happens. Typically, we begin to feel a shift on our horizon at around age 57, as the realization settles in that we will soon be 60. We may initially feel a sobering reality about this number, as thoughts of our own mortality begin to arise. For some, the idea of retirement is not too far off, or perhaps we fear being made "redundant." And while some look forward to the freedom that retirement will bring, others begin to worry about financial security and stability, hoping that they've saved enough to see themselves through the time they have left. Health issues also begin to show up around this age, and many have faced significant loss by now, through divorce or the death of parents, family, or friends. Some will become grandparents, stepping into a new role that can bring both wonder and a shift in identity.

Once again, Saturn marks another milestone of maturity, a turning point where we are called to reassess our values. We may be acutely aware that there is no turning back—we are now truly on the road to elderhood, and although we are not yet "old" and our lives still contain untold possibility, we are crossing a threshold that can bring fear and anxiety as we face this uncharted territory. Many come to this juncture with some measure of trepidation and fear that this time will bring depression, stagnation, and stasis, but it does not have to be so. While it is true that we now step into a different phase of life, viewing it through an archetypal lens can be a deeply spiritual way to align with this rite of passage.

While aging is one of the most natural consequences of being born into a physical body, Western culture is not always kind or supportive of this inevitability. Although this passage can be challenging to all genders, it can be particularly difficult for people who identify as women. In a misogynistic patriarchal culture in which appearance and youth are equated with worth, approaching 60 can come with some difficult feelings. Women have long reported that after a certain age, they begin to feel invisible. Youth and beauty carry privilege and receive validation. As a society, we are bombarded on a regular basis with media images depicting young and sexually desirable women. And while previous generations also contended with the media's portrayal of its current ideal, this generation must grapple with their own self-image juxtaposed with an impossible ideal to live up to without the intervention of plastic surgery and injectables. And while there are now more "women of a certain age" portrayed in magazines and commercials, their image is often used to sell antiaging products. Further, these images are again an ideal that is difficult to embody in the real world without intervention that goes beyond antiaging creams. The message is that salon-perfect silver hair and fine smile lines are permissible, but a sagging jawline is not.

By the second Saturn return, most women have reached menopause, which brings hormonal changes that effect many aspects of life, including appearance. As much as we might balk at being superficial, seeing these changes reflected in our mirror is a stark reminder that we are not as young as we once were. It is important to normalize the grieving process many of us feel when confronted with the reality of aging. And like with all grief, we are not meant to be stuck there forever but to find meaning in it. Our task is to come to a place of loving self-acceptance. Over the last few years, more women have been allowing their hair to go naturally gray. Personally, I see this as an act of cultural resistance, as it begins to expand and re-envision the narrow, media-constructed beauty ideals that are damaging at any age.

However, aging is a deeply personal process for everyone. Whether we choose to embrace our silvers or we feel better with the occasional visit to the derma clinic, there should be no judgment. Although we are no longer young, this can be an exciting time to reinvent the way we show up in the world. What image do we want to project? Once we get past the idea that the only form of beauty is youth, we can experiment with myriad styles and looks that represent our evolving identity. We are not generic older people, nor do we ever have to be, whatever age we are lucky enough to attain. We are a treasure trove of experiences and memories that we alone can claim. One can be interesting, beautiful, and youthful at any age, and charm and creativity know no age limit.

Although we have returned to the story "Vasilisa the Beautiful," at this point in our lives we no longer relate to the coming-of-age motifs of the original protagonist in the story. Our perspective has shifted, and we are coming of age in another way. And while we are still far from elderly, it is now time to begin to understand the mysteries of Baba Yaga. Baba Yaga is a Crone goddess, and in Jungian terms, Saturn is connected to the archetype of the *Senex*, or the wise elder. Saturn is aligned with those deities who exemplify the wisdom that comes with age and maturity, such as An Cailleach, "the old woman of winter" from the Gaelic lands; Hecate in her aspect as the Crone at the Crossroads; Frau Holle, the ancient Teutonic goddess of winter; and of course, the Russian Baba Yaga. Saturn resonates with the wisdom of the elders, passed-down traditions, time-honored ways of knowing, and our psychic ancestral bones.

However, instead of being viewed as a source of wisdom and Keeper of the Mysteries, the Crone is often seen as a subject to be feared. She has seen it all, nothing phases her, and she has earned wisdom about life's cycles. To the uninitiated, her uncanny ways of knowing might seem suggestive of magical power. The Crone has long been associated with the witch, and it should come as no surprise that during the witch hunts that swept Europe in the early modern period, most of the victims were older women. The Crone is also closer to death and the otherworld, and in a youth-obsessed culture, death and aging are a frightening reminder that someday we are all going to face that great unknown. In a collective in which anyone can appear as a so-called wisewoman because they have the right aesthetic and a certain amount of social media followers, the wisdom of age and experience can be marginalized. We must remember discernment, to look beneath the visage and see behind the veil. Because she has seen it all, the Crone suffers no fools. She tells it like it is and calls us out when necessary, and for those with fragile egos, this can be threatening.

Like Saturn, Baba Yaga is both initiator and gatekeeper, reminding us that "to know too much too soon can make one grow old before their time." She teaches us that one must work for the light of wisdom. One must do what is required before they are permitted to the next phase of initiation. As a wise teacher, she sets Vasilisa a series of tasks, both mundane and magical, and although the lessons behind these tasks may not be immediately apparent, Baba Yaga knows that we each need to learn the basics before we can move to the next stage. Like Saturn, she promises reward for hard work, focus, and discipline and threatens consequences if we avoid it. Perhaps surprisingly, Baba Yaga's hut is filled with earthy abundance: stocked larders, jars full of healing herbs, and other creature comforts, suggesting she herself has done the work and earned the rewards that come with experience and perseverance. She is the stern, sometimes fierce, but always wise teacher. After Vasilisa has performed the tasks set out for her, she is granted the lantern in the dark, the ancestral skull that will see her through the next stage of her becoming.

Regardless of gender, the second Saturn return is the time to distill our life experience, embrace Baba Yaga, and reclaim our inner witch. The work now is to contemplate all that we have learned and integrate it into a potent decoction that is ours alone to make. While you may share similar life experiences with others—not another soul, living or dead, has ever lived the story that is your life.

Although autumn is not the intoxicating perfume of spring, it has its own rich beauty. I went out to my witch's garden this October morning to see that the mugwort and skullcap had produced another crop since July. At the same time, the leaves on the oak had transformed to dazzling shades of scarlet, amber, and carnelian as daylight has faded and the sun has set a little earlier each night. My friend, the esteemed herbalist and homeopath Seraphina Capranos, describes the mysterious interior journey that occurs in plants during autumn: "This time of year in the northern hemisphere is marked by the vital force moving downward and inward, into the roots of the plants. In herbal medicine roots reach deep into our body, breaking up stagnation, and guiding us to what needs attention."[63] The turning within that occurs in nature during autumn is reflected in our own lives as we reach the rite of passage that is the second Saturn return. We too are called "downward and inward" on a journey of inner alchemy as we reflect and contemplate the distance we have traveled. And although we are no longer in the first flush of springtime in our lives, there is still potential for growth and harvests yet to be gathered.

Despite the challenges of this threshold, the second Saturn return is a reminder to live in the present. There is a tremendous freedom in no longer being as concerned with what others think, as we become more comfortable speaking our truth, even when that truth is inconvenient or unpopular. We have likely stopped comparing ourselves with others as much, on- and offline. There is a self-acceptance that can accompany this transit, as the passing years have helped us develop a deeper appreciation for who we truly are, and we've learned to become more self-forgiving. Those who have spent years taking care of others are learning to prioritize their own needs and set healthy boundaries on their time and resources. The little things don't bother us as much anymore as we become aware of how ephemeral life is. Our self-awareness has grown, and we may feel more grounded and centered than ever before. As Saturn is about releasing and paring down, this can be a time for letting go of the past, including resentments and self-limiting beliefs. We are deepened and richer for all our expe-

---

63. Seraphina Capranos, personal communication with the author, October 15, 2020.

riences, and our life becomes a tapestry woven with substance and meaning.

Although there is a natural turning within that happens around this time, it is paradoxically a time of new beginnings. We are given an opportunity to take stock of the way we have consciously or unconsciously structured our life and turn over a new leaf. The realization that life is finite, and that time seems to move more quickly with every passing year, can be a catalyst to do those things we've always wanted to do. While many look forward to retirement, it's not uncommon for others to explore their passions and begin a new career at this stage. With every generation, the perception of 60 changes as life expectancy increases. The average 58-to-60-year-old today is much younger mentally and physically than ever before, and as I write this, a whole new generation is quickly approaching its second Saturn return. Beginning in 2023, the very first wave of those known as Generation X will come to this threshold, bringing their own experiences and changing the face of what it means to age at this time in history.

Chapter 21

Navigating Your Second Saturn Return

At this time, it's common to find yourself in deep reflection, spontaneously reviewing your life, and it can be highly therapeutic to record your reflections. There are many reasons to write your story. As I explained at the beginning of this book, reclaiming your story is a way to re-enchant your life, to see your unique journey through an archetypal lens with you as the protagonist. Although one can begin to write their story at any point, it is often at the second Saturn return that we feel called to witness the many layers that have shaped our life. Writing your memoir can help you recognize your accomplishments, reframe limiting beliefs about life and Self, and make sense of the past. It can help you embrace your truth and honor your resilience. It can be a teaching tale for others. It can also help you recapture the moments tucked away in memories that you want to treasure forever. Writing your story can help you heal and transform as you prepare to move into the next chapter of your life. It can be helpful at this stage to go back to your previous crossroads (first Saturn return and Midlife Transits) to recall the turning points, life events, and personal milestones that have shaped your story so far. Turn to the table of contents to find the age ranges for these previous crossroads times and reflect on what was happening for you during those years. For those who are not sure that astrology "works," I guarantee you will be surprised at what you find.

Revise Your Bucket List

What have you always wanted to do that has been left undone? Now's your chance to rethink what's important to you now and make space for the things that give your life meaning. What gave your life meaning 20 or 30 years ago may have changed since you have grown. It might be as simple as spending more time doing the things you enjoy, or it could be that you want to travel more. Perhaps you've always wanted to write a book, take art classes, or learn Italian. You may wish to become an activist, bringing your passion and experience to benefit people with less privilege. Maybe you want to go to graduate school or travel to the world's power places, such as Machu Pichu, Glastonbury, or Newgrange. Perhaps you've always wanted to trace your roots and explore the land and culture of your ancestors. You may wish to have a courageous conversation with someone or write a letter that you may or may not send. Don't censor yourself or think of all the reasons why you can't experience the things you long for. Write your dreams down anyway. Sometimes, when we dare to speak them aloud and commit them to paper, life has a way of surprising us. This is called magick.

Palliative care nurse and author Bronnie Ware explains that the most common regret expressed by the dying is "I wish I'd had the courage to live a life true to myself, not the life others expected of me." Ware recorded her observations of people in their last three weeks of life in her book, *The Top Five Regrets of the Dying: A Life Transformed by the Dearly Departing*. She shared with *The Guardian*, "This was the most common regret of all. When people realise that their life is almost over and look back clearly on it, it is easy to see how many dreams have gone unfulfilled. Most people had not honoured even a half of their dreams and had to die knowing that it was due to choices they had made, or not made."[64]

Although your life is not "almost over," this is sobering stuff. Your second Saturn return is an opportunity to clarify your core values and sense of purpose. This will take some self-reflection, and because the Saturn return often also coincides with periods of alone time, you will likely have no shortage of opportunities to drop down and do some serious soul searching. Remember that you are in a time of profound transition. What was important to you even a short while ago might be waning as you move toward a new sense of self. It could take some time for insight to arise, so be patient with yourself. You are exactly where you are supposed to be.

Become a Mentor

By the time you have reached this rite of passage, you have gained a lot of self-knowledge and life experience that can help guide others. Your story may be just what someone needs to hear that will change their life. There are many ways one can be a guide, and while career mentorship is quite common, a mentor can bring perspective to any area of life. Parents with grown children can provide guidance to new parents. Seasoned writers can give advice to aspiring writers. Those who have experienced loss can be a light in the dark for those newly acquainted with it. The ways in which your knowledge and experience can make an impact in someone else's life are myriad. During this passage, it's common to start thinking of passing down the torch in some way. Sometimes we take our stories for granted, and sharing our insight with others can help us realize how valuable our experience is. I am reminded of the Hermit in the tarot, the wise guide standing atop a mountain, bearing the lantern to light the way for those who are not as far along on the path.

---

64. Susie Steiner, "Top Five Regrets of the Dying," *Guardian*, February 1, 2012, https://www.theguardian.com/lifeandstyle/2012/feb/01/top-five-regrets -of-the-dying.

Take Care of Your Health

As we age, taking good care of ourselves mentally, emotionally, and physically is more important than ever. Once again, Saturn is associated with aging, but especially with bones, the skeleton, and teeth—the very structure of our physical being. Strength training and staying physically active can help build bone density. The enamel on our teeth begins to wear down as we age as well, so consider adding calcium, vitamin D, and magnesium supplements to your daily routine to help keep bones and teeth strong, and don't put off that visit to the dentist. Quitting smoking can reduce your chances of smoking-related cancers and heart disease. If you find yourself becoming a bit forgetful, explore plant allies such as lion's mane mushroom that can help with focus, memory retention, and attention. And if it's been awhile since you got yourself to the mat, Alyssa Shaffer writes, "Studies have shown that doing yoga is one of the greatest ways to slow the clock. And it's not just because you're helping your muscles remain limber—a regular yoga practice may increase the levels of stay-young hormones that can slow the aging process."[65] Take a look at your diet and exercise routine and make sure it's supporting you to live your best life. This is a great opportunity to talk to your doctor or alternative health practitioner for ways you can keep young and healthy at this stage and beyond.

Embrace Your Inner Witch

Whether you've been a practicing witch for decades or are new to embracing your inner witch, you are now at the peak of your power and wisdom. Nearly 35 years ago when I was a witchling and fledgling astrologer, I could not wait to be older so people would take me more seriously. I studied and worked magick and learned astrology at the feet of my teachers, but no matter how much I practiced, I knew

---

65. Alyssa Shaffer, "How Yoga Can Help You Look Younger Than Your Years," *Health*, last modified January 11, 2017, https://www.health.com/fitness /yoga-workout-anti-aging.

the vital ingredient that was missing could only be attained with life experience and the passage of time. And while I had already made a descent to the underworld early in life, Saturn's unwavering lesson is that it takes time to integrate what we learn in those shadowy places. Our ego may be under the illusion that we can rush Saturn's teachings, but by now we know the truth. I recently did an interview for a podcast, and the interviewer referred to me as "an elder witch." I laughed out loud, momentarily shocked by her words. And then I realized that it was in fact true. Although I still have a few years until my own second Saturn return, in the way of crossroads transits, I can already feel it on my horizon.

If you are new to the way of the witch, it need not be daunting. You can embrace your inner witch by observing the cycles of the moon. Mark the days on the Wheel of the Year, and get to know the spirits of place where you live. Create an altar. Do your own shadow work and reclaim the lost fragments of your soul. Learn to read tarot or to interpret your birth chart. Read reputable books on witchcraft and astrology or take a course in herbalism. Study mythology and folklore. Learn the history of the witch in early modern Europe. Explore the traditions of the witch through your own ancestral lineage. Plant a garden and tend it by the cycles of the moon, and learn the mysteries of communicating with plants. Spend more time in nature, whether it be at the ocean's shore, the forest, or the dessert. Take time to reflect on your own life and note the times when your intuition was spot on or you focused so intently on something that it came to pass.

Those who have done the inner work, those who have come to the edge of the abyss not once but multiple times, those who have gone into the dark and faced Baba Yaga, Ereshkigal, and their own shadow—whether or not they call themselves so—know the way of the witch. If this is you, embrace your inner witch and know that you have been truly and properly initiated into the mysteries through the cycles of Saturn, our life's greatest teacher. Your intuition has been honed by experience and time. You have likely known both devastating loss and the regenerating power of joy, and like Baba Yaga, you know something of the cycles of birth, death, and rebirth. And while we may find ourselves on the edge of the dark wood once again, by now we are learning the terrain. Although the entrance looks slightly different from when we last came this way, the path will be familiar. We may even feel a strange sense of excitement as we step forward into this next rite of passage. We have earned the keys that unlock the mysteries of the hut of Baba Yaga.

Journal Reflections for Your Second Saturn Return

- Think back to your first Saturn return around age 30. How have you changed, grown, or been tested since then? Who have you become?

- What do you know now that you didn't know then?

- Choose a story line in your life, especially one that seems to repeat in different ways. Can you identify the archetypal themes at play?

- Reframe your story to this point as if you were the protagonist/hero. What knowledge have you acquired because of what you've gone through in your life?

- What message(s) would you share with others based on your own unique experiences?

- What does aging mean to you? Do you have fears about aging, and if so, how can you reframe them?

- How will you embrace your inner witch?

- How does it feel when you think of taking on the mantle of power and stepping into your sovereignty? Do you feel any resistance?

A Magickal Tool Kit for Your Second Saturn Return

Saturn is a potent magickal ally to work with as you approach your second Saturn return. By the time we have come to this rite of passage, we have a deeper understanding of the sacred dimensions of Saturn than ever before. Work magick with Saturn to connect with the wisdom of the elders, and explore the uncanny layers of Crone magick. Call on Saturn to say goodbye to old chapters, let go, and release, as well as to step across new thresholds and into your power. Rituals for self-forgiveness and acceptance are enhanced by Saturn. You can also connect with Saturn for grief and closure rituals as you move into a new phase of life. No matter what you're facing, Saturn can help you gain clarity and see the reality behind the illusion. See the Saturn correspondences at the end of this chapter for more ways to work with Saturn as a magickal ally.

Pathworking: Embracing the Baba Yaga

To become wise, it takes a capacity for self-reflection and the courage to learn from our experiences. At this crossroads we have the choice to lean gracefully into the next phase of our becoming and embody the wisdom of our years or to allow ourselves to become embittered by our experiences. Becoming rigid or fearful or endlessly repeating unhelpful patterns is the shadow of the Elder archetype. We must recall that Saturn can show up in his guise as the Devourer, or he can be the god of harvest.

When we arrive at this juncture, we carry within us the knowledge of both spring and autumn. Like a perennial plant that breaks through the soil of winter each year with new green shoots, embedded in our psyche is the consciousness of beginning. And paradoxically, although it is autumn in our lives, we know instinctively how to start anew. We realize now that there is magic in every season. Instead of feeling jealous or envious of the younger generation, we can connect with our younger self and summon compassion for earlier versions of who we were as we now know how much we did not know. We have witnessed the cycles, and if we have done our work, we know instinctively that it is time to step over the threshold into the next phase. Like Baba Yaga, we have learned when to be kind and when we must show our teeth and be fierce. We have come to a place in our lives when we have begun to understand sovereignty. And, once again, we find ourselves sorting the seeds. Baba Yaga knew the value of this task when she assigned it to Vasilisa, because it is a task we must return to again and again over the course of our lives as we separate what contains the potential for growth and what does not. Our mission now is to keep growing, keep asking questions, brave the unknown, and most of all, find meaning in our story.

The following pathworking is best done at night on the waning moon or when the Moon is in Capricorn or Scorpio. It can be helpful to reread the pathworking for the first Saturn return beginning on page 69. Find a quiet place where you will be undisturbed for about fifteen to twenty minutes and turn off your phone. Ground and center in your preferred way and clear the space by burning herbs, essential oils, or incense (check the correspondences for Saturn for ideas). Wear unrestrictive clothing and get into a comfortable position. Use pillows for support if needed and a blanket to keep warm and comfortable. If challenging emotions arise during this pathworking, check in with yourself. Have a journal and a pen ready to write about feelings that come up.

The sun has just passed through the gateway of autumn equinox, the time of year when day and night are of equal balance. You sense this subtle shift and inhale the scent of woodsmoke, ripe berries, and decaying leaves, evoking old memories deep in the body. You find yourself on the edge of a dark forest. The last rays of the setting sun are leaning gracefully toward the approaching dark, igniting the glowing skin of the birches with luminous gold. You step across the threshold and enter the wood. Leaves crunch underfoot, and rings of Amanita muscaria glow in the deepening shadows. There is a strange familiarity about this place. You are sure you have come this way before, but something has changed. You hear hoofbeats, and nearby a rider in black crashes past you through the underbrush.

An enormous harvest moon rises behind the trees. You have been walking for a long time when you approach a crossroads. A raven's hoarse cry echoes through the wood and is answered by another. Pausing, you decide to turn left. You walk deeper into the forest until you come to a curious little hut surrounded by a fence of bones. It has been a long time since you were last here, and you are tired. You don't remember being this tired the last time you made this journey. But then you were uncertain, afraid. Now, you inhale deeply, steadying yourself, as a strange sense of expectation and excitement wells up inside you.

Before you can utter a word, an old woman's voice comes from inside the hut: "I know you. Why have you come?"

You pause for a moment and answer, "I seek your wisdom once again, Grandmother." The door of the hut opens, and out steps the old woman. She narrows her eyes and sighs, "Yes, I suppose it is time." Muttering to herself, she waves you inside, but you try the gate, and it is locked. For a moment, you are still. Perhaps this time the portal will not open. The old woman stands patiently on the porch, hands on hips, waiting. You reach your hand into your pocket and find the key that she gave you so many years ago. You fit it into the lock and turn it. The pins tumble, and the gate creaks open. The old woman nods, and her face creases into what could almost pass for a smile. You take a deep breath and step across the threshold.

You ascend the steps and enter the hut. It looks much the same as before. A fire is crackling in the grate and on the counter sits a mortar and pestle alongside baskets of forest medicine. She motions for you to sit, and you pull out a chair at the old wooden table and rest your weary legs. She pours a cup of tea from the kettle and hands it to you. You take the cup in both hands and inhale the fragrance of dark spices, herbs, woodsmoke, and something else that you cannot quite name. You look down at the cup, and the light from the Full Moon shines through the window and illuminates the surface of the dark steaming brew like a mirror. From far away, the old woman speaks, "What do you see?"

The steam swirls and parts, and you catch a momentary glimpse of your reflection. You see the story of your life written on your face, the telltale furrows where heartbreak burrowed in and left its signature. Crinkles etch the corners of your eyes from every time you laughed so hard that tears ran down your face and your sides ached. The steam gathers again, and you see yourself walking through the dark wood the first time you came this way. You see yourself tentatively approaching the little hut, with its fence made with the bones of the ancestors. You are younger, and your face is smooth and unlined—before you crossed that first threshold. And then another. And then another. Before you unlocked each gate that led you through the story of who you have become. The steam swirls again as you watch the unfolding scenes of all the years that have brought you to the present moment. The images rise and fall, and you see yourself once again walking through the dark forest. Your face is deeply lined and wrinkled. The pale light of a waning moon casts little light, and it is difficult to see the path. And although you see yourself walking slowly through the snow, supported by an oaken staff, your expression is serene, and your step is sure. You know the way. The old woman steps out on the porch and greets you like an old friend. She waves you up the stairs, and into the hut. It is much like before. There is a fire crackling in the grate, and a mortar and pestle sit on the counter beside baskets that overflow with herbs and mushrooms. You sit at the table, and the old woman pours a cup of tea for you, and a cup for herself. "So," she says, her face creased with a broad grin, "tell me everything."

The steam clears, and you hear the sound of hoofbeats. You open your eyes, and it is morning. The old woman is grinding fragrant herbs with the mortar and pestle, and a fire is crackling in the grate. You rise and thank her and walk outside. The sky is just beginning to pale, and the first frost of the season sparkles in the last light of the setting moon. She follows you to the gate and presses the key in your hand. "There are still gates to unlock."

Ritual: Taking on the Mantle

When you come to the threshold that is your second Saturn return, you are stepping into a new level of wisdom, power, and inner knowing. Whether you saw them as such at the time, you have undergone countless initiations over the course of your life, and now it is time to integrate all that you've learned so you can take on the mantle of the Wisewoman or Sage. Taking on the mantle is to step into your power and sovereignty, to take on a position of leadership in a sense, the role of the mentor or Wise One in your community or family. Of course, one does not simply arrive at this age and automatically become wise, but if you have done your inner work, contemplated the story of your life, and engaged in self-reflection, you will have likely developed the ability to perceive the patterns beneath the surface of things and learned to listen to your intuition. You are becoming increasingly aware of your own power to influence and transform your own life and the collective. This ritual is best done on the Full Moon or when the Moon is in Capricorn or Scorpio.

You Will Need

- A cloak or shawl
- Baba Yaga's Tea (see page 222)
- Pictures of yourself around your first Saturn return (age 28–30) and subsequent crossroad times throughout your life
- One candle for each picture (tealights work well)

- Drumming music or a drum if you have one
- Mirror
- Journal and pen

You may want to spend some time finding the right cloak or shawl for this ritual, as this will be your mantle of power from this day forward. You will be able to don this cloak whenever you need to connect with your wise inner self, whenever you are feeling less than or not enough. It is a reminder that you are a being of power, wisdom, magic, and experience. You might already have something perfect for this purpose in your closet, but if not, peruse the charity shops and consignment stores first. There are incredible pieces out there that might be just what you are looking for. Before you go out, set your intention that you will find the most beautiful mantle that is meant for you. When you find this glorious piece, it's important that you properly cleanse and consecrate it for your purpose. Burn herbs or incense connected to Saturn (see pages 223–24) and "bathe" the piece in the smoke. If the cloak has a residual smell from its last owner or from being stored for a long time, you can sprinkle baking soda on it and hang it up outside in the sunshine if weather permits. This can take from a few hours to a few days. If it takes more than a day, be sure to take the mantle inside overnight so it doesn't become damp. The baking soda will help absorb any lingering odors and further purify the garment. Alternatively, you may wish to have something special made for this purpose or buy something new. Once you have cleansed and conse-crated your mantle, you are ready to begin the ritual.

Brew Baba Yaga's Tea. Turn on drumming music or have your own drum close at hand. Set up your altar with tea, the mantle, photos, and any Saturn correspondences, such as stones or specific colors that you wish to include. Cleanse your working area and create sacred space by burning essential oils, herbs, or incense associated with Sat-urn. If your tradition includes casting a circle, do so now. Stand or kneel before your altar and breathe in for the count of four, hold for the count of four, and breathe out for the count of four. Repeat this slow, measured breathing until you have come to a place of relaxation and feel centered. You may wish to rock or sway gently to the cadence of the drums to further enhance a light trance state. If you have your own drum, take it up and start a slow beat. Turn your attention to the earliest picture of yourself on your altar and recall that moment in time. Who were you then? What was important to you? What were your struggles and what did you learn? What were you proud of? What do you know now that you did not know then? If you could go back in time and speak to your younger self, what would you say? Dialogue with that earlier version of yourself. Forgive yourself for any mistakes and for not knowing. Thank yourself for the commitments you made and for all the lessons you learned so you could become the person you are today. Light the candle in front of the picture and say, "I forgive you. I thank you. I honor you." Turn to the next photo and contemplate who you were at that time. Forgive yourself for any mistakes that you made and remember you would not be who you are today if your younger self knew all the answers. What would you say to your younger self if you could go back in time with what you know now? Light the candle, and say, "I forgive you. I thank you. I honor you." When you have dialogued with each picture, gaze into the mirror at your reflection. Summon compassion and truly witness the being who looks back at you. A being of experience, courage, and wisdom. A being who has been shaped by life like a sculpture from raw clay. A being with a unique story that has never been lived in quite the same way ever before.

Take the mantle off your altar and place it around your shoulders. Take a deep breath: this is the mantle of power, and you have earned the right to wear it. Gaze at your reflection and behold who you have become. Reflect for a moment on all those who have crossed this threshold before you. It is now your turn to wear the mantle of the

Wise One. Take the cup of Baba Yaga's Tea in both hands, hold it before you, and say,

Of who I once was and who I've become
The distance I've traveled, to the beat of my drum
I honor my path and all I've achieved
I witness the past and all that I've grieved
By standing stone and herbs that heal
By birch and earth and Solomon's seal
I take in the wisdom of those who have passed
And take on the mantle of power at last

Close your eyes and drink the tea slowly. Make sure to taste it in all its complexity. Contemplate the wisdom of the Elders: Baba Yaga, An Cailleach, the ancestors. Do they have a message for you now? It can be a word, an image, a symbol. Feel the comforting weight of the mantle around your shoulders, lending gravity, dignity, and protection to this important rite of passage. Visualize the mantle glowing, becoming part of you by right of all you have learned in your life to this point. Sit quietly and consider how far you have come. When you are ready, write down any insights that have come to you. Take as long as you need. When you are done, rise and extinguish the candles, and close the circle if you have cast one. Come back into your body by moving gently and perhaps eating something. Know that you have crossed an important threshold and are subtly changed as you prepare to move into the next chapter of your life.

Baba Yaga's Tea

You Will Need

- Small piece of ginger root
- 2 parts birch bark
- 1 part dried Solomon's Seal
- Small cinnamon stick
- 3–4 cloves

A good guideline is to use approximately 1 teaspoon dried herbs per 1 cup water. Bring water to a boil. Chop the ginger roughly. Add all the herbs and turn down the heat to a simmer for 15 to 20 minutes. Strain the herbs and pour ½ cup to drink. If you are unfamiliar whether any herb is right for you, check with an herbalist.

Allies and Correspondences for Saturn Times

STONES AND MINERALS: Anthracite (coal), black tourmaline, diamond, epidote, fluorite, fossilized bone, jet, obsidian, smoky quartz, stibnite

FOR GRIEF OR A BROKEN HEART: Emerald, lepidolite, peridot, rhodonite, rose quartz

FOR ENERGY: Bloodstone, carnelian, fire agate, garnet, Herkimer diamond, ruby, sunstone, zircon

ESSENTIAL OILS: Douglas fir, pine, vetiver, cypress, oakmoss

FOR UPLIFTING AND ENERGIZING: Cinnamon, ginger, clove, bergamot, cardamom, basil, juniper, peppermint, dragon's blood, spearmint, benzoin, tangerine, sweet orange, rosemary, frankincense, myrrh

DEITIES: Saturn, Kronos, Baba Yaga, Hecate, Frau Holle, An Cailleach, the Norns, the Dagda

COLORS: Black, gray

HERBS: Henbane,* datura,* wolfsbane,* monkshood,* angelica, burdock, comfrey, black hellebore, mullein, shepherd's purse, Solomon's seal, holly, witch hazel, juniper, elderberry (*Indicates baneful plants. These plants are highly toxic, and great care and research should be taken before working with them in any capacity, including handling them.)

PLANT ALLIES FOR SUPPORT: St. John's wort, lemon balm, milky oats, ginseng, *Ginkgo biloba*, schisandra berries, cordyceps, holy basil, maca, hops, eleuthero root, golden root, white oak bark

BACH FLOWER REMEDIES FOR SUPPORT: Wild oat, aspen, beech, cerato, chestnut bud, clematis, elm, gentian, hornbeam, larch, mimulus, mustard, oak, olive, rock rose

SIGNS: Capricorn, Aquarius

HOUSE: Tenth

ELEMENT: Earth

TAROT CARD: The Devil

Conclusion

No matter what juncture you are at in the unfolding story that is your life, and whether or not you happen to be currently navigating one of life's crossroads, know that you are in sacred territory. Every moment is a cocreation with the universe, an opportunity to re-enchant your life and find meaning and magic in the very act of being alive.

May whatever passage you find yourself in bring you home to yourself.

Blessings on your quest.

Glossary

Aspect: The mathematical angle, or relationship, made between two (or more) points in a birth chart, including planets or other important points in the chart, such as the ascendant or midheaven. Some aspects are considered easy and harmonious, such as trines and sextiles, while others are potentially challenging, such as the square or opposition. The major aspects are the conjunction (0 degrees), opposition (180 degrees), square (90 degrees), trine (120 degrees), and sextile (60 degrees). We each have aspects in our birth chart that describe patterns within our psyche, and as the planets move, they also form aspects to the planets in our birth chart, which are called transits.

Degree: The unit of measurement in a natal chart. The chart is a circle containing 360 degrees, which symbolizes the ecliptic. The ecliptic is divided into 12 signs, containing 30 degrees each, from 0 to 29.

House: The chart is divided into 12 sections, or houses. The chart begins with the cusp of the first house, otherwise known as the rising sign, and is read counterclockwise from that point. When you were born, each planet was in a specific house and sign, or in a different part of the sky in relation to the time and place of your birth. Each house represents a different life area, such as health and wellness, career, relationships, and more. While your birth chart stays the same, planets move across the ecliptic and transit your birth chart, changing houses and bringing up different themes at given times in your life.

Orb: Although we can time when transits will be exact, they are considered within orb a few degrees before and after they reach that exact degree. Orbs can vary slightly depending on the planets in question, but a good guideline is approximately 5 degrees on either side of the exact degree of a given aspect or transit. This means that even though a transit might not be exact, you will likely still be feeling its effects while it is within orb.

Retrograde: When a planet appears to move backward in relation to the earth. Planets do not actually move backward—it's a matter of perception, an optical illusion. All planets except the Sun and Moon go retrograde at different times. In astrology when a planet is retrograde, it is a symbolic period of time that is associated with confusion, mix-ups, or backtracking in the area that the planet rules. Retrogrades can be ideal times for reflection, slowing down, and pausing before moving forward.

Transit: One of the fundamental ways to forecast timing and trends in astrology is the interpretation of the movement of the planets in the sky as they transit planets in the natal chart. When a moving planet approaches the degree of a planet or point in our chart, it is forming an aspect to that planet. We would look at what aspect is forming, as well as the archetypal character of the planets involved to get an idea of what kind of energy is at play. Further, we can look to the houses in our chart that those planets are transiting to understand the life area that might be affected.

Bibliography

Alighieri, Dante. *The Divine Comedy.* Vol. 1. Translated by Henry Wadsworth Longfellow. Boston: Fields, Osgood & Co., 1871.

BBC News. "Oldest Lunar Calendar Identified," October 16, 2000, http://news.bbc.co.uk/2/hi/science/nature/975360.stm.

BBC News. "'World's Oldest Calendar' Discovered in Scottish Field," July 15, 2013, https://www.bbc.com/news/uk-scotland-north-east-orkney-shetland-23286928.

Bolen, Jean Shinoda. *Gods in Everyman: Archetypes That Shape Men's Lives.* 25th ed. New York: HarperCollins, 2014.

Boyne Valley Tours, "Newgrange.com," accessed November 18, 2020, https://www.newgrange.com/.

Brown, Brené. "Own Our History. Change the Story." *Brené Brown* (blog), June 18, 2015. https://brenebrown.com/blog/2015/06/18/own-our-history-change-the-story/.

Campbell, Joseph. *The Hero with a Thousand Faces.* 3rd ed. Novato, CA: New World Library, 2008.

Campion, Nicholas. *Astrology and Cosmology in the World's Religions.* New York: New York University Press, 2012.

Culpeper, Nicholas. *Culpeper's Complete Herbal.* Edited by Steven Foster. New York: Sterling, 2019.

Estés, Clarissa Pinkola. *Women Who Run with the Wolves: Myths and Stories of the Wild Woman Archetype.* New York: Ballantine, 1992.

Forrest, Steven. *The Changing Sky: Creating Your Future with Transits, Progressions and Evolutionary Astrology*. 2nd ed. Borrego Springs, CA: Seven Paws Press, 2002.

———. *The Inner Sky: How to Make Wiser Choices for a More Fulfilling Life*. Borrego Springs, CA: Seven Paws Press, 1988.

Forrester, Sibelan, trans. *Baba Yaga: The Wild Witch of the East in Russian Fairy Tales*. Edited by Sibelan Forrester, Helena Goscilo, and Martin Skoro. Jackson: University Press of Mississippi, 2013.

Gary, Gemma. *Traditional Witchcraft: A Cornish Book of Ways*. 10th anniv. ed. London: Troy Books, 2019.

Gimbutas, Marija. *The Language of the Goddess*. New York: HarperCollins, 1989.

Goss, Theodora. "Heroine's Journey: The Dark Forest." *Theodora Goss* (blog), December 17, 2014. https://theodoragoss.com/2014/12 /17/heroines-journey-the-dark-forest/.

Greene, Liz. *The Astrological Neptune and the Quest for Redemption*. York Beach, ME: Samuel Weiser, 1996.

———. *The Astrology of Fate*. Boston, MA: Weiser, 1984.

———. *Saturn: A New Look at an Old Devil*. York Beach, ME: Weiser, 1976.

Hand, Robert. *Planets in Transit: Life Cycles for Living*. Atglen, PA: Whitford Press, 1976.

Harris, Russ. *The Confidence Gap: A Guide to Overcoming Fear and Self-Doubt*. Boston, MA: Trumpeter, 2011.

Hobson, Nick. "The Anxiety-Busting Properties of Ritual." *Psychology Today*, September 25, 2017. https://www.psychologytoday.com /ca/blog/ritual-and-the-brain/201709/the-anxiety-busting -properties-ritual?collection=1108996.

Hollis, James. *Finding Meaning in the Second Half of Life: How to Finally, Really Grow Up*. London: Gotham Books, 2005.

Hopcke, Robert. *A Guided Tour of the Collected Works of C. G. Jung*. Boulder, CO: Shambhala Publications, 1999.

Jacobsen, Thorkild. *The Treasures of Darkness: A History of Mesopotamian Religion*. New Haven: Yale University Press, 1976.

Johnson, Robert A. *Owning Your Own Shadow: Understanding the Dark Side of the Psyche*. New York: HarperCollins, 1991.

———. *We: Understanding the Psychology of Romantic Love*. New York: HarperCollins, 1983.

Jung, C. G. *Psychology and Religion*. Vol. 11 of *Collected Works of C. G. Jung*. New Haven, CT: Yale University Press, 1938.

———. *Symbols of Transformation*. Vol. 5 of *Collected Works of C. G. Jung*. Princeton, NJ: Princeton University Press, 2014.

Kennedy, Maev. "Stonehenge Bones May Be Evidence of Winter Solstice Feasts." *Guardian*, December 20, 2009. https://www.theguardian.com/culture/2009/dec/20/stonehenge-animal-bones-solstice-feast.

Kessler, David. *Finding Meaning: The Sixth Stage of Grief*. New York: Scribner, 2019.

Kimmerer, Robin Wall. *Braiding Sweetgrass: Indigenous Wisdom, Scientific Knowledge, and the Teachings of Plants*. Minneapolis, MN: Milkweed Editions, 2014.

Lüthi, Max. *Once Upon a Time: On the Nature of Fairy Tales*. Bloomington: Indiana University Press, 1976.

Markway, Barbara, and Celia Ampel. *The Self-Confidence Workbook*. Emeryville, CA: Althea Press, 2018.

Martin, Clare. *Alchemy: Soul of Astrology*. Swanage, UK: Wessex Astrologer, 2020.

National Geographic. "Chichén Itzá." November 15, 2010. https://www.nationalgeographic.com/travel/world-heritage/article/chichen-itza.

NicMhacha, Sharynne MacLeod. *Queen of the Night: Rediscovering the Celtic Moon Goddess*. York Beach, ME: Red Wheel/Weiser, 2005.

O'Donohue, John. *To Bless This Space Between Us: A Book of Blessings*. New York: Doubleday, 2008.

Perera, Sylvia Brinton. *Descent to the Goddess: A Way of Initiation for Women*. Toronto: Inner City Books, 1981.

Plath, Sylvia. *The Bell Jar*. London: Faber and Faber, 1977.

Sasportas, Howard. *The Gods of Change: Pain, Crisis, and the Transits of Uranus, Neptune and Pluto*. Swanage, UK: Wessex Astrologer, 2007.

Shaffer, Alyssa. "How Yoga Can Help You Look Younger Than Your Years." *Health*. Last modified January 11, 2017. https://www.health.com/fitness/yoga-workout-anti-aging.

Steiner, Susie. "Top Five Regrets of the Dying." *Guardian*, February 1, 2012. https://www.theguardian.com/lifeandstyle/2012/feb/01/top-five-regrets-of-the-dying.

Stritof, Sheri. "Estimated Median Age of First Marriage by Gender: 1890 to 2018." The Spruce. Last modified December 1, 2019. https://www.thespruce.com/estimated-median-age-marriage-2303878.

Sullivan, Erin. *The Astrology of Midlife and Aging*. New York: Penguin, 2005.

———. *Saturn in Transit: Boundaries of Mind, Body and Soul*. York Beach, ME: Weiser, 2000.

Tarnas, Richard. *Cosmos and Psyche: Intimations of a New World View*. New York: Plume, 2006.

Trees for Life. "Oak Mythology and Folklore." 2020. https://treesforlife.org.uk/into-the-forest/trees-plants-animals/trees/oak/oak-mythology-and-folklore/.

Turner, Toko-pa. *Belonging: Remembering Ourselves Home*. Salt Spring Island, BC: Her Own Room Press, 2017.

Ware, Bronnie. *The Top Five Regrets of the Dying: A Life Transformed by the Dearly Departing.* Carlsbad, CA: Hay House, 2012.

Weller, Francis. *The Wild Edge of Sorrow: Rituals of Renewal and the Sacred Work of Grief.* Berkeley, CA: North Atlantic Books, 2015.

Welwood, John. *Toward a Psychology of Awakening: Buddhism, Psychotherapy, and the Path of Personal and Spiritual Transformation.* Boulder, CO: Shambhala Publications, 2000.

Wheeler, Post. *Russian Wonder Tales.* New York: Century Company, 1912. https://openlibrary.org/books/OL7236461M/Russian -wonder_tales.

Windling, Terry. "On Illness: In a Dark Wood." *Myth & Moor* (blog), October 17, 2019. https://www.terriwindling.com/blog/2019 /10/on-illness-in-a-dark-wood.html.

Wolkstein, Diane, and Samuel Noah Kramer. *Inanna, Queen of Heaven and Earth: Her Stories and Myths from Sumer.* New York: HarperCollins, 1983.

To Write to the Author

If you wish to contact the author or would like more information about this book, please write to the author in care of Llewellyn Worldwide Ltd. and we will forward your request. Both the author and the publisher appreciate hearing from you and learning of your enjoyment of this book and how it has helped you. Llewellyn Worldwide Ltd. cannot guarantee that every letter written to the author can be answered, but all will be forwarded. Please write to:

Danielle Blackwood
℅ Llewellyn Worldwide
2143 Wooddale Drive
Woodbury, MN 55125-2989
Please enclose a self-addressed stamped envelope for reply,
or $1.00 to cover costs. If outside the U.S.A., enclose
an international postal reply coupon.

Many of Llewellyn's authors have websites with additional information and resources. For more information, please visit our website at http://www.llewellyn.com.

Notes

Notes

Notes

Notes

Notes